THE SEVEN GIFTS OF THE HOLY SPIRIT

KEVIN VOST, PSY.D.

THE SEVEN GIFTS
OF THE HOLY SPIRIT

EVERY SPIRITUAL WARRIOR'S
GUIDE TO GOD'S INVINCIBLE GIFTS

SOPHIA INSTITUTE PRESS
MANCHESTER, NEW HAMPSHIRE

Sophia Institute Press
Box 5284, Manchester, NH 03108
1-800-888-9344

www.SophiaInstitute.com

Sophia Institute Press® is a registered trademark of Sophia Institute.

Library of Congress Cataloging-in-Publication Data

Names: Vost, Kevin, author.
Title: The seven gifts of the Holy Spirit : every spiritual warrior's guide
  to God's invincible gifts / Kevin Vost, Psy.D.
Description: Manchester, New Hampshire : Sophia Institute Press, 2016. |
  Includes bibliographical references.
Identifiers: LCCN 2016040102 | ISBN 9781622824120 (pbk. : alk. paper)
Subjects: LCSH: Gifts, Spiritual—Catholic Church. | Catholic
  Church—Doctrines.
Classification: LCC BT767.3 .V67 2016 | DDC 230/.2—dc23 LC record
available at https://lccn.loc.gov/2016040102

To all the clergy, religious, and laity
who teach the Faith:

May the Holy Spirit guide you
and bless you with His gifts.

CONTENTS

PREFACE

Wherefore as sin is opposed to virtue from the very
fact that a man sins, there results a diminution of that
good of nature, which is the inclination to virtue.

St. Thomas Aquinas, *Summa Theologica*, I-II, Q. 85, art. 1

The gifts are bestowed to assist the virtues and
to remedy certain defects ... so that, seemingly,
they accomplish what the virtues cannot.

St. Thomas Aquinas, *Summa Theologica*, I-II, Q. 68, art. 8

While researching for a biography of St. Albert the Great in 2011,
I came across an earlier biographer's declaration that within an
author's first book can be found the kernels of all of his subsequent
works. Upon a little reflection, I found that this sure is true for me,
as the kernels contained in *Memorize the Faith!* (Sophia Institute
Press, 2006) have popped into all kinds of subsequent books.

You see, one of the seeds in *Memorize the Faith!* was chapter
5, "The Seven Virtues" (four cardinal and three theological virtues), that four years later would grow into the book *Unearthing
Your Ten Talents* (Sophia, 2010) (having sprouted three additional, intellectual virtues in the process). Five years later, lo
and behold, chapter 4 of *Memorize the Faith!*, "The Seven Capital
Sins," had grown into *The Seven Deadly Sins* (Sophia, 2015).

Well, another year has gone by, and now it is time to reap what was sowed in *Memorize*'s chapter 13, "The Seven Gifts of the Holy Spirit," with this book that you hold in your hands. I hope you will find that it was a good crop.

In explaining the growth of the early Church at Corinth, St. Paul wrote: "I planted, Apollos watered, but God gave the growth" (1 Cor. 3:6). Well, as far as this book goes, I planted it with Sophia Institute Press publisher Charlie McKinney's gracious permission; it was watered by many at Sophia, including Michael Lichens, Nora Malone, and Sheila Perry;[1] and if this book should help any readers attain any spiritual growth, well, we'll chalk that up to the Holy Spirit, the all-loving Giver of all the gifts that matter the most.

Now, as for the gist of this particular book, in some ways it is the complement and completion of *The Seven Deadly Sins*, both in its subject matter and in its Thomistic approach.[2] As I wrote in *Unearthing Your Ten Talents*, contrasting St. Thomas Aquinas's approach to man with that of some schools of modern psychology:

> Christians know that none of us is without sin. Because of the Fall, we all are prone to sin and imperfection, though this was not our original intended state. We can experience lust and hurtful anger and a myriad of other impulses to sin,

---

[1] These people work painstakingly, by the way, to weed out all the errors and typos I do not spot in the fields of my text. Chances are, though, that some will still remain. My goal is to write a book that could earn a *nihil typos*, although I doubt that I'll see that in this life!

[2] Although you need not have read that book to profit from this one.

but through Jesus we can receive the grace to overcome them. We need not live out our lives at the level of our sin and weakness. Christians know that the violent, lustful, selfish *id* is not *really* us. St. Thomas Aquinas knew all about fallen man's sinful side, but he was certainly no Freudian pessimist regarding human nature. He was not so interested in how low we can go, as in how high we can rise.[3]

In *Unearthing Your Ten Talents*, I focused primarily on the *virtues*, those perfections of our powers that allow us to rise, and briefly introduced the gifts of the Holy Spirit, gifts that we could say *perfect those very perfections and help us rise as high as we can go*—all the way to heaven, God willing! Here, in this book, the gifts themselves take front and center stage as we unwrap them so that we may enjoy and share them.

Well, I suppose you have the general gist of this book's place in the scheme of things now. There's so much to cover in the chapters ahead that I'll conclude right now with a few words from Scripture (prose that perhaps every author who produces a preface should prayerfully peruse and put into practice):

And so, methinks, it is here; to expiate, to digress, to indulge in curiosity on every point, is for the arch-historian; your epitomist will ask leave to such brevity, and let long disquisitions be. And now, to our matter! Here is preface enough; it were ill done to draw out the preamble, and leave our story cramped for room. (2 Mach. 2:31–33, Ronald Knox Edition)

---

[3] Kevin Vost, *Unearthing Your Ten Talents: A Thomistic Guide to Spiritual Growth* (Manchester, New Hampshire: Sophia Institute Press, 2010), 7–8.

INTRODUCTION

SEVEN GIFTS THAT ARE OUT OF THIS WORLD

Now it is manifest that human virtues perfect man according as it is natural for him to be moved by his reason in his interior and exterior actions. Consequently man needs yet higher perfections, whereby to be disposed to be moved by God. These perfections are called gifts, not only because they are infused by God, but also because by them man is disposed to become amenable to divine inspiration.

—St. Thomas Aquinas, *Summa Theologica*, I-II, Q. 68, art. 1

WHAT IS THE WORLD'S GREATEST GIFT?

If we focus on the word "world's" in the question "What is the world's greatest gift?", I'd say that the greatest of all "worldly" gifts is the God-given capacity to attain earthly happiness. As Aristotle argued and St. Thomas Aquinas confirmed, happiness is the final end, or the ultimate thing that we seek on earth. Everything else we seek, be it pleasure, honor, fame, or the like, is sought because we think it will make us happy. Now, to be happy on earth, we need to exercise fully our God-given powers as beings created in His image with intellect and will, so that we are not drawn instead to frustration and possibly to self-destruction by blindly following our sensual appetites. The perfections of our rational powers that can rein in our sensual desires and lead us to true happiness are called natural virtues.

Now, if we change our focus a bit to consider not merely what is "of the world" but anything that exists in the world, even if it comes from beyond this world, we move into a realm beyond even earthly happiness and the natural virtues that lead us to it. As natural virtues perfect our rational powers, there is a class of gifts from above that perfect the very virtues themselves. That is the realm and those are the gifts that this book explores, as we seek to find and obtain the greatest of all gifts in the world—and far beyond it! That greatest of all gifts bar none is the bliss of the eternal beatific vision of God that we'll experience in heaven, and the seven gifts we'll examine within these pages are the gifts that God gave us to help us get there!

These glorious gifts, with a small g, come to us from the Gift with a capital G. They are the gifts of the Gift Himself, that is, the seven gifts of the Holy Spirit. Let us, like the child in us who can't wait for Christmas (or, in this case, Pentecost), take a quick peek under their wrappings. Many who know these gifts only by name may have little clue as to what glorious gifts they are.

- *Fear of the Lord:* Although some modern secularists argue that it demeans human dignity and suggests an immoral God who would want us to fear Him, there is so much more to this gift that begins with a painful awareness of our human limitations and vulnerability, but culminates in the deepest of love for a God who sustains us and offers us the greatest of gifts on earth as well as His presence in heaven.

- *Piety:* The word *piety* may connote a kind of pharisaical self-righteousness that looks down on others, or it may call forth images of people absorbed in pious devotions, bordering on superstition, and oblivious to more central lessons of Christ. Through the gift of piety, however, we see others as our brothers and sisters, and God as our loving *Abba,* Father.

- *Knowledge:* Pope St. John Paul II explained in his great encyclical on faith and reason[4] that some Christians adhere to a kind of "fideism," a belief that faith alone is all we need to guide us to truth without due regard for reason and knowledge. Many secularists cling to a

---

[4] *Fides et Ratio,* September 14, 1998.

"scientism" that believes that worldly science, divorced from anything divine, will lead us into all the truth we ever need. Little do adherents to fideism and scientism know, however, that from the very virtue of faith flows the Holy Spirit's gift that would guide us to ever deeper realms of knowledge[5] to discern God's truths about ourselves and all of His creation.

◆ *Fortitude:* We sometimes hear the term *intestinal fortitude* applied to those who have what we call "guts." By the natural virtue of fortitude, we can overcome obstacles that keep us from the good while we endure hardships along the way. By the Holy Spirit's gift of fortitude we can fight the good fight, regardless of the obstacles, even, if God should allow it, unto the martyrdom that will bring us eternal reward.

◆ *Counsel:* How popular it is in our day to question all authority as we sing about doing it our way. Who needs counsel, after all, when we are entitled to have our own opinions (unless, of course, *your* opinion offends *my* sensibilities!)? Little do we who are so wise in our own eyes[6] realize how badly we are in need of the gift of counsel so that the Holy Spirit may guide us to do things *His* way!

---

[5] As to the joined etymological roots of *science* and *knowledge*, the English word *science* derives from the Latin word *scire*, "to know." Indeed, in various translations of ancient and medieval Catholic writers, the virtue of knowledge is sometimes called the virtue of science.

[6] See Proverbs 3:7: "Be not wise in your own eyes; fear the LORD and turn away from evil" and Isaiah 5:21: "Woe to those who are wise in their own eyes, and shrewd in their own sight!"

- *Understanding:* Although there are profound mysteries like "the peace of God, which passes all understanding" (Phil. 4:7), the Holy Spirit's gift of understanding lifts us beyond our human powers of understanding and gives our intellects the light to peer deeper into the supernatural truths of the Faith.
- *Wisdom:* Philosophy is the love (*philos*) of wisdom (*sophia*). It is the realm within human reason that can point us toward ultimate truths, but the wisdom received from the Holy Spirit takes us beyond human reason, that we may not only grasp higher truths but may savor and cherish them and use them to guide our actions.

WHY A THOMISTIC (AND BONAVENTUREAN) APPROACH?

Readers of my previous books will not be surprised by this book's Thomistic approach, since it was the "Thom" of the Thomists, St. Thomas Aquinas (1225–1274), Angelic Doctor of the Catholic Church and patron saint of scholars, whose wisdom brought me back to the holy doors of the Church after twenty-five years in an atheistic wilderness. His truly good and beautiful syntheses of the blessings of both faith and reason have guided all of my works since then (at least that was my intention!). This book, however, is thoroughly Thomistic in many other ways.

St. Thomas Aquinas has provided the foundational treatment of the gifts of the Holy Spirit, among the most complete and thorough explanations in the two-thousand-year history of Christianity. And in these pages, every theme, not to mention a great deal of content, borrows from our saintly scholar's treatment in his writings, specifically his peerless *Summa Theologica*.

Thomas, in contrast to some other theologians, was the greatest theological champion of the gifts of the Holy Spirit as *distinct from* and *aimed at the perfection of the virtues*.

When we examine the scriptural basis of the gifts, the Holy Spirit as Love and Gift, the special charisms of the Holy Spirit, the natural and theological virtues, the gifts themselves, the gifts in their relationship to the Beatitudes and to the fruits of the Holy Spirit, we are following Thomas's lead, for he addressed in breadth and depth every one of those subjects. In fact, let me show you next how thoroughly our approach to the gifts will follow the path laid out by St. Thomas Aquinas, whom we could call, without fear of exaggeration, a gift of the Holy Spirit to the Holy Catholic Church!

Here then, is the subject matter of our chapters as addressed in the *Summa Theologica*, so that you might see where our plan for this little book arose within the big book that gave rise to it. (Feel free to use the accompanying tables to guide you to where you can dig deep and drink deeply from St. Thomas's own well of wisdom on each and every subject we will address.)

Beyond St. Thomas's great influence on me, and his having laid out all of our topics for us, this book is Thomistic in a third and no less important sense. St. Thomas is known as the greatest integrator and synthesizer of holy wisdom with whom God has graced the world. Never seeking to be novel for novelty's sake, or to promote himself, St. Thomas possessed an amazing intellectual humility and docility eager and open to learning the truth, regardless of its source. All his works are suffused with scriptural wisdom, and his writing shows such a profound respect for the writings of the ancient Church Fathers that in 1879 Pope Leo XIII, citing the sixteenth-century cardinal, Dominican master general, and Thomist Thomas Cajetan, declared that St. Thomas had "inherited the intellect" of them all.

Thomas sought wisdom as well in the writings of pagan philosophers such as Aristotle, Cicero, and Seneca; in Jewish philosophers such as Maimonides; and in the Arabs Averroës and Avicenna, although he always exercised the utmost care in separating the wheat of truth from the chaff of error in their writings. So, it is in this third sense that our approach is Thomistic in spirit. Within each chapter we will seek out and acknowledge wisdom on our subject from many sources, including those who lived after St. Thomas.

Among the most prominent and helpful sources we will examine are spiritual conferences or collations presented by none other than the great Dominican's great Franciscan friend and peer, the Seraphic Doctor, St. Bonaventure. Like the Angelic Doctor, the Seraphic Doctor combs the Scriptures and writings of the great Church Fathers, Doctors, and saints to bring us fascinating and edifying insights of his own. As we move through the chapters on each of the gifts, we'll savor some Seraphic insights on each one.

Another spiritual master whose treatment of the gifts rivals the completeness of St. Thomas's treatment (and borrows most openly from it) is that of Denis the Carthusian (1402–1471), who provides a wealth of penetrating perspectives on the seven gifts as seen through Carthusian lenses.

The book perhaps closest to this one in spirit and in structure is one by John Poinsot (1589–1644), a Dominican who so dearly loved Thomas that he is known to posterity as John of St. Thomas![7]

---

[7] These books will all be duly named and referenced when we draw from their wisdom in the pages ahead.

Others closer to our time who have written complete works on the seven gifts and whose wisdom we will freely seek and share include the Benedictine Prosper Louis Pascal Guéranger (1805–1875), the Anglican priest turned Catholic Father Henry Formby (1816–1884), Mexico City's archbishop Luis M. Martinez (1881–1956), and the Jesuit cardinal Carlo Maria Martini (1927–2012).

So there in a nutshell is the Thomistic and Bonaventurean gist of this book as far as its overall themes go. Let's zoom in now and introduce this book's most important feature, the plan we will employ to understand better the supernatural nature and to enjoy the spiritual benefits of the gifts of the Holy Spirit.

SUBMISSION PLANS!

We are employing a Thomistic and Bonaventurean approach to the seven gifts of the Holy Spirit for the very practical goal of finding the very best means to unwrap, enjoy, and share their fruits with others! Readers of my *Seven Deadly Sins*[8] will note the parallel to that book's "Battle Plans" section, in which we put on the armor of Christ to vanquish vice and sin. Our plans here, though, are called "Submission Plans," for to employ these most powerful of all gifts, we must learn to submit our wills humbly and docilely to the stirrings of the Holy Spirit, who will gird us for spiritual battle with invincible, supernatural gifts.

We will unwrap the gifts one by one so that we may better understand them, enjoy the succulent spiritual fruits they bring

---

[8] Sophia Institute Press, 2015. (Indeed, very attentive readers will note that the subheadings in this introduction parallel the subheadings of that book's introduction too.)

into our lives, and share their fruits with our neighbors. We will address them in ascending order, from the lowest (although still utterly magnificent!) to the highest, as a ladder that the Holy Spirit provides to enable us to climb to heaven. This order turns upside down the order in which they are presented in Scripture as they descend from the Holy Spirit upon man.

Our submission plans will be in the form of the following:

1. Grasping the gifts
2. Embracing the sacraments
3. Examining our thoughts and deeds for obstacles to the gifts
4. Practicing prayer
5. Cultivating virtues, beatitudes, and fruits
6. Flying to our Mother's aid
7. Imitating Christ

Each submission plan will be specifically developed and applied to each gift in its individual chapter.

PROFILES IN GIFTEDNESS (AND TWO BONUS GIFTS)

Another feature you will find at the end of each chapter is a gift box of sorts, a brief "Profile in Giftedness" essay. All saints possessed, enjoyed, and shared all seven of the gifts, but some clearly stand out as exemplary models of particular gifts, and even the briefest look at their lives can help bring the gifts to life for us. (As you read each chapter, you might consider whether a particular saint comes to your mind as a model of that gift and then see at the end of the chapter if that is the saint I had in mind.)

A second set of bonus gifts come courtesy of the Spirit-filled intellect of St. Thomas Aquinas. Here in "Angelic Analysis" essays, we will present very briefly some of the crucial philosophical and theological issues the Angelic Doctor addressed in some depth so that a rich and full grasp of the meaning and significance of each gift would ring out loud and clear. These issues include the scriptural basis of the gifts, the reason the Holy Spirit has been given the names of "Love" and "Gift," and the relationships and distinctions between the seven gifts of the Holy Spirit and the special charisms, virtues, beatitudes, and fruits (the stuff of our second master table).

Finally, each chapter will conclude with a "Profile in Grace" essay providing an example of a saint or a sage who, in important ways, *personified and lived* the related gifts and graces of God considered in the Angelic Analyses. To give you a little foretaste, I ask you to ponder these questions:

- Which saint might you think is most closely linked to the scriptural account of the seven gifts of the Holy Spirit?
- Can you think of a saint so giving that his or her name could almost be "Gift"?
- Whom did St. Thomas consider the greatest prophet in the Old Testament — and why?
- Which pagan philosophers might best represent the heights of natural virtue in their lessons and in their lives?
- Which saint before Thomas most completely laid the groundwork for our understanding of the seven gifts?
- What blessed person did Saint John Paul II declare "a man of the beatitudes"?
- Which saint filled an entire nation with the fruits of the Holy Spirit?

You'll find the answers to all of these questions in each chapter's last essay.

LASTING THINGS LAST

The Seven Deadly Sin's introduction ended with a section entitled "Last Things Last," which noted that the concluding chapter would address the deadliest of all sins and how it can be subdued by the highest of all virtues. We will end this introduction with "Lasting Things Last," since we will recall in the last chapter how St. Thomas demonstrated that these seven gifts of the Holy Spirit will never lose their value but will last forever, after they help us obtain our salvation and while we experience eternal and beatific bliss with God. We will emphasize too our call to share their fruits with our neighbors in the hopes that they too might enjoy these gifts with God in eternity.

With an end like that in store for us and for our loved ones, God willing, shall we not then begin to unwrap these seven gifts that forever keep on giving?

MASTER TABLE FOR FURTHER READING ON EACH GIFT IN THE *SUMMA THEOLOGICA*

1. Fostering Fear of the Lord	II-II, Q. 19: Of the Gift of Fear
2. Practicing Piety	II-II, Q. 121: Of the Gift of Piety
3. Acknowledging Knowledge	II-II, Q. 9: Of the Gift of Knowledge
4. Fortifying Fortitude	II-II, Q. 139: Of the Gift of Fortitude

SEVEN GIFTS THAT ARE OUT OF THIS WORLD

5. Counting on Counsel	II-II, Q. 52: Of the Gift of Counsel
6. Unwrapping Understanding	II-II, Q. 8: Of the Gift of Understanding
7. Welcoming Wisdom	II-II, Q. 45: Of the Gift of Wisdom

MASTER TABLE FOR CHAPTER-END ESSAY MATERIAL

1. The Gifts in Sacred Scripture	Scattered throughout the *Summa Theologica*. See notes in the chapter.
2. The Holy Spirit as Love and Gift	I, Q. 37: Of the Name of the Holy Ghost, as Love
	I, Q. 38: Of the Name of the Holy Ghost, as Gift
3. The Special Charisms of the Holy Spirit	I-II. Q. 111: Of the Division of Grace
4. The Virtues in General	I-II, Q. 55: Of the Virtues, as to Their Essence
The Intellectual Virtues	I-II, Q. 57: Of the Intellectual Virtues

The Cardinal Virtues	I-II, Q. 61: Of the Cardinal Virtues
The Theological Virtues	I-II, Q. 62: Of the Theological Virtues
5. The Gifts in General	I-II, Q. 68: Of the Gifts
6. The Beatitudes	I-II, Q. 69: Of the Beatitudes
7. The Fruits of the Holy Spirit	I-II, Q. 70: Of the Fruits of the Holy Ghost

But those who indeed burn to know the truth and are avid
to obtain grace; those whose minds are enlightened and
whose love is pure, want above all to have books which
while exciting devotion will at the same time adorn the
intellect with divine knowledge. This is the mode in which,
in this present tract, I will endeavor to discuss the gifts of
the Holy Spirit. This I will strive to do, so far as the Holy
Spirit, God sublime and blessed above all things, may deign
to help me. This is the way in which the Catholic Doctors
of old used to write.... And this mode of writing is renewed
in modern Doctors: Thomas, Albert, Aegidius and others.

—Denis the Carthusian, *Gifts of the Holy Spirit*

SURRENDER PLANS FOR SUBMITTING TO THE HOLY SPIRIT'S GUIDANCE

If you wish to have the love of the Son, and of
the originating Principle, and of the Gift that is
the Holy Spirit, dispose yourself for grace.

—St. Bonaventure, *Collations on the Seven Gifts of the Holy Spirit*

Through the fear of the Lord, we rise to piety, from piety
then to knowledge, from knowledge we derive strength,
from strength counsel, with counsel we move toward understanding, and with intelligence toward wisdom and thus, by
the sevenfold grace of the Spirit, there opens to us at the
end of the ascent the entrance to the life of Heaven.

—Pope St. Gregory the Great, *Homily on the Prophet Ezekiel*, 2, 7, 7

Come Holy Spirit, fill the hearts of your faithful and enkindle in them the fire of your love. Heavenly King, Con-
soler Spirit, Spirit of Truth, present everywhere and filling
all things, treasure of all good and source of all life, come
dwell in us, cleanse and save us, you who are All-good.

—*Catechism of the Catholic Church*, no. 2671

WHEN SURRENDER LEADS TO VICTORY

Readers of my *Seven Deadly Sins* may note a parallel here, for in the former book we examined "Battle Plans for Conquering the Seven Deadly Sins," while here we examine "Surrender Plans for Submitting to the Holy Spirit's Guidance." This by no means suggests that we've decided to surrender and give up in our fight against sin! In both books we seek to "put on the whole armor of the Lord" (Eph. 6:11) and wage battle against our sinful natures, but in this book our focus is especially on armor and weapons entirely beyond human nature, for the gifts provide armor that is explicitly "of the Lord," deriving directly from the Holy Spirit. It will be as if we are reinforcing our chain mail and steel plating with an impenetrable force field—but only if we can learn to surrender and submit to the Holy Spirit!

To obtain the stoutest armor and the sharpest weapons that come from the Holy Spirit's gifts, we must do as St. Bonaventure has advised and dispose ourselves to grace. We must adopt a kind of *active passivity*, we might say—*passive* in that we become docile and open to the Holy Spirit's stirrings, willing to follow wherever He leads, but *active* in our cooperation with His holy guidance, willing to put one foot in front of the other in order to follow Him on the path that He lays out for us.

As we saw in our quotation from Pope St. Gregory the Great, and as we'll flesh out in the chapters ahead, the gifts of the Holy Spirit, when arranged in order from the least to the greatest, form, as it were, a ladder up to heaven.[9] So, we will employ a metaphorical ladder of sorts — two, in fact, if we consider the arrangement of the order of the gifts a spiritual ladder of its own.

Here are the seven steps of our ladder that we'll use to ascend to each of the gifts of the Holy Spirit:

SEVEN STEPS TOWARD UNWRAPPING, ENJOYING, AND SHARING THE SEVEN GIFTS

1. Grasping the nature of each gift
2. Embracing the sacraments
3. Rooting out obstacles that hinder our use of the gifts
4. Practicing prayer
5. Cultivating related virtues, beatitudes, and fruits
6. Flying to our Mother's aid
7. Imitating Christ

So let us begin our spiritual ascent with a quick jump to the fourth rung of our ladder, as we prepare to delve into the seven glorious gifts of the Holy Spirit with a prayer invoking the Gift-Giver Himself:

Come, Holy Spirit, fill the hearts of Your faithful and kindle in them the fire of Your love. Send forth Your Spirit and they shall be created. And You shall renew the face of the earth.

---

[9] St. Robert Bellarmine (1642–1721), in his *Summary of Christian Doctrine*, explicitly compared the seven gifts to a ladder, the bottom step resting on the earth with the spirit of fear of the Lord and the last step touching heaven through the spirit of wisdom.

*O God, who by the light of the Holy Spirit, did
instruct the hearts of the faithful, grant that by the same
Holy Spirit we may be truly wise and ever enjoy His
consolations. Through Christ our Lord. Amen.*[10]

---

[10] See *Catechism of the Catholic Church: With Modifications from the Editio Typica* (New York: Doubleday, 1997), nos. 2670–2672.

CHAPTER 1

FOSTERING FEAR OF THE LORD

Filial fear holds the first place, as it were, among
the gifts of the Holy Ghost, in the ascending order,
and the last place in the descending order.

—St. Thomas Aquinas, *Summa Theologica*, II-II, Q. 19, art. 9

It seems to me that the fear of the Lord is a very beautiful tree planted in the heart of the holy person and watered
continuously by God. And when that tree has grown to
its fullness, that person is worthy of eternal life.

—St. Bonaventure, *Collations on the Seven Gifts of the Holy Spirit*

THE GIFT OF FEAR TRUMPS ANY PRESENT UNDER THE TREE!

If we are to enjoy and share gifts, as we all know from our childhood experiences of Christmas, the first thing we must do is unwrap them. Can you recall for a moment your excitement in those early years? Admit it now too: Did you ever, when no one else but perhaps a trusted friend or sibling was with you, pick up those gifts, feel their heft in your hands, shake them a bit and listen to them, hold them up to strong light, or even, heaven forbid, unwrap them and then wrap them back up? Well, the gifts that the Holy Spirit has prepared for us are far more exciting, more worthy of unwrapping, cannot be outgrown, and will last far beyond any earthly lifetime. Happily too, they have already been unwrapped for us by two thousand years of the greatest minds of the Catholic Church—inspired by the Gift Giver Himself!

This is our first step, then, with the first gift of the Holy Spirit that we will examine in depth, yet still only scratch the surface. We will come to grasp just what these gifts are so that we may know how fully we've been blessed and may surrender to the Holy Spirit, who has such great plans in store for us. We will start with the word *fear* itself. St. Denis the Carthusian, citing St. Augustine, tells us that fear is "avoidance of future evil,"[11]

---

[11] Denis the Carthusian, *Gifts of the Holy Spirit*, trans. Ide M. Ni Riain (Dublin: Columba Press, 2013), tract III, art. 41.

from which we might gather that although the emotion of fear is not something pleasant that we typically seek out, we certainly do hope to avoid future evil, so if fear can help us do that, then it surely can be a good thing after all.

There is much to understand regarding fear in its several forms, and we'll begin with the kinds of fear St. Thomas Aquinas has been so kind as to catalog for us. Here they are in brief:

FOUR FORMS OF FEAR PER ST. THOMAS AQUINAS
1. *Worldly fear*: fear of loss of earthly goods or pleasure
2. *Servile fear*: fear of punishment
3. *Initial fear*: fear blending servile and filial fears
4. *Filial fear*: fear of committing a fault and offending God

Worldly fear is no gift of the Holy Spirit. It refers to our natural fears of losing the material goods or the sensual pleasures we desire and encountering privation, frustration, or physical pain instead. Neither is this kind of fear "the beginning of wisdom" (Ps.111:10). Jesus Himself advised us, "Do not fear those who kill the body but cannot kill the soul" (Matt. 10:28). It is by abandoning our worldly fears that we can focus our attention on a proper fear of the Lord: a fear infused with love, a fear lest we become less than what is fitting for creatures made in God's image.

What St. Thomas, drawing on the writings of Sts. Paul and John (Rom. 8:15; 1 John 4:17–18) and of the Church Fathers, calls *servile* fear is the lowest form of the Holy Spirit's gift of fear of the Lord. This is the fear of transgressing the laws of God out of a desire to avoid punishment. It is far from a perfect fear, in that it is not inspired by the love of God for His own sake, but its object—the avoidance of God's displeasure and subsequent punishment—is good.

Initial fear derives from the Latin *initium*, "beginning." As the beginner starts to grow in a healthy fear of the Lord, *servile* fear and *filial* fear (a more perfect form of fear) might both be present. A man beginning to grow in charity, for example, might do the right thing both because he loves justice *and* because he fears to be punished for misdeeds. As his love for justice grows with time, his servile fear of punishment will fade away. As we read in 1 John 4:18, "Fear has to do with punishment, and he who fears is not perfected in love." Further, "perfect love casts out fear."

As we grow in love, then, servile fear diminishes, and the increase of *filial* fear, the last and most perfect form, leads to the perfect wisdom of charity. Filial, or *chaste*, fear, conjoined with charity, is akin to the fear and deference that a son gives to his father or a wife to her husband out of affection and love. The object of this fear is the avoidance of committing a fault, of failing to live up to God's expectations for us. And here again we see St. Thomas's awareness of the potential for human spiritual growth and development.

Seven hundred years after St. Thomas wrote the *Summa Theologica*, when modern psychologists began building theories of the development of moral reasoning, they started with the avoidance of punishment at the bottom rung of the moral ladder, leading to concepts of perfect justice and love at its top. Indeed, St. Thomas calls us to strive continually to better ourselves, to develop our virtues with the aid of the gifts and make ourselves complete, for the greater glory of Him who made us. A healthy filial fear should inspire us all the more to develop our God-given capacities for His honor and glory. Further, we should always recall what the modern psychological theorists do not consider, that by the gifts of the Holy Spirit, starting with fear of the Lord, our moral acts are ultimately perfected by something beyond our psychological powers—namely, the motion of the Holy Spirit Himself.

Now let's turn to the Seraphic Doctor to get our first taste of how this great saint can help us win and unwrap the gift of fear of the Lord. I'll start with a couple of winning pairs of threes. St. Bonaventure asks: "But what value is there in fearing God? Tobit 4:23 states: 'Do not be afraid, my son. Indeed, we live a poor life. But if we fear God, we will have many good things.'"[12] He then goes on to explain three of those "good things," three effects or advantages of the fear of the Lord, of which I'll merely provide a few highlights with my own parenthetical comments:

THREE ADVANTAGES OF THE FEAR OF THE LORD PER ST. BONAVENTURE

1. "The first advantage of the fear of God, I say, is that it *opens us to the influence of divine grace*."[13] St. Bonaventure provides scriptural references from Isaiah 66:2, Psalm 146:10–11, and Philippians 2:12–13 and also includes a lengthy citation from St. Bernard of Clairvaux, including this line: "In truth, I have learned that nothing is as helpful for procuring, preserving, and increasing the grace of God as having the fear of God at all times." (Recall how fear of the Lord is the first step up the ladder of the gifts. It is the first step in opening our souls to the channel of all the Holy Spirit's graces.)

---

[12] St. Bonaventure, *Collations on the Seven Gifts of the Holy Spirit*, trans. Zachary Hayes, O.F.M. (St. Bonaventure, NY: Franciscan Institute Publications, 2008), p. 57.

[13] Ibid.; italics added.

2. "Second, the fear of God is important in *introducing the rightness of divine justice*. Sirach 1:27–28 states: Fear of the Lord drives out sin; for the person without fear cannot be justified."[14] (The gift of fear of the Lord recognizes the gravity of sins against God and the justice of God's punishments if we do not repent.)

3. "Third, the fear of God is important for *obtaining the illumination of divine wisdom*, since 'the beginning of wisdom is fear of the Lord.'"[15] He clarifies that "servant-fear" (servile fear) is the beginning of wisdom, "but does not remain with wisdom." The "fullness of wisdom" comes from "the fear of filial reverence." (We may note here the compatibility of the Thomistic and Bonaventurean approaches to the gift of fear of the Lord.)

Well, there is one pair of threes. Let us look at the Seraphic Doctor's second winning pair, this trio being "concerned with the perfection of the fear of the Lord."[16] St. Bonaventure notes that the perfection of the gift of fear consists in these three things.

THREE PERFECTIONS OF THE FEAR OF THE LORD PER ST. BONAVENTURE

1. The first perfection of the fear of the Lord is that of "perfect holiness or cleansing of conscience."[17] Citing texts from 2 Corinthians 7:1, Sirach 2:20–22, and Romans 2:4–5 on the need to cleanse ourselves from defilement and prepare our hearts by penance, Bonaventure

---

[14] Ibid., p. 59.
[15] Ibid.; see Ps. 110:10; Sir. 1:16; Prov. 9:10.
[16] *Collations*, p. 62.
[17] Ibid.; italics added.

declares that those who fear the Lord will apply discipline to themselves and cease from sinning.

2. The second perfection of fear of the Lord consists of "the perfect readiness to obey."[18] He cites from 2 Chronicles 19:7, "Qoheleth" (Ecclessiastes) 7:19, and Deuteronomy 10:12–13, verses that indicate that those with fear of the Lord do all of God's things diligently, neglect nothing, keep the whole law, and summing up, quoting Qoheleth 12:13: " 'Fear God and keep God's commandments. This makes the human person to be complete.' This is to be perfect. Therefore, if you wish to be perfect, fear God."[19]

3. The third component of perfect fear of the Lord is "complete firmness of trust."[20] The fear of the Lord brings such a trust in God that earthly fears are overcome. St. Bonaventure cites Psalm 90:5–6, which notes that God's truth surrounds us like a shield so that we will not be afraid of the terrors of the night and the arrows that fly by day, and Proverbs 14:26, which says that the fear of the Lord is a tower of strength. Then he notes that "the person who truly fears God has something that no one can take away. One who fears something other than God has something that ought to be taken away."[21]

Now that we've unwrapped the kinds of fear we may experience, the nature of the fear of the Lord that is the gift of

[18] Ibid., p. 63.
[19] Ibid.
[20] Ibid.
[21] Ibid., p. 64.

the Holy Spirit, and its advantages and perfections, we need to examine what we can do to acquire, hold on to, enjoy, and share this great gift.

HOW THE SACRAMENT OF BAPTISM SETS US A-SAIL TOWARD HEAVEN

The seven sacraments were given to the Church by Christ, and through them the graces of the Holy Spirit flow into our souls. Indeed, in the first Sacrament of Initiation, Baptism, we are blessed with the gifts of the Holy Spirit. These include the gift of fear in its initial state, with its potential to blossom through charity into the kind of reverential, filial fear that brings to us such good things as we've seen (e.g., openness to divine grace, justice, and wisdom; cleansing of conscience; perfection of obedience; and complete firmness and trust in God).

All the gifts, including fear of the Lord, are fortified further in the sacrament of Confirmation, when the bishop calls upon the Holy Spirit to fortify, guide, and assist us by strengthening in us the seven gifts that will help us become more like Christ.

There's a role here for the sacrament of Reconciliation as well. When we truly repent and our sins are forgiven in the sacrament of Penance, we are reconciled to God, the channel of His grace is again wide open for us, and the wind of the Holy Spirit is ready to fill our sails, if we are willing to keep from rowing in the wrong direction! Moreover, St. Bonaventure notes that as our conscience is purified, we will dread even venial sins.

HOW *NOT* TO EMBRACE THE GIFT OF FEAR

So let's say we have made a full and honest confession. (Think back to your last one. Didn't your soul feel so good?) We walk out of the confessional and perform our prescribed penance. Our sins have been forgiven, and our soul has been cleansed and reopened to the graces of God.

If we seek to remain in the embrace of those graces, particularly the gift of fear, we need to take action to keep our thoughts, feelings, desires, and deeds amenable to the stirrings of the Holy Spirit. Indeed, we need to make sure that we are not actively working against it. We oppose this gift directly when we choose to ignore God's loving mercy toward us, failing to nurture our filial fear. We also oppose it when we choose to ignore the potential of God's just punishments when we do not exercise even an appropriate servile fear, having declared our own wills the master. We will see this in ourselves when our earthly fears predominate and we worry about acquiring all the pleasurable things in life while avoiding all struggle and pain.[22]

Some may miss the mark of a proper fear of the Lord in another way, not by ignoring or devaluing it, but through the excessive misplaced zeal of *scrupulosity*. Our fear of the Lord should open our hearts and minds to all of the other gifts, not paralyze us in morbid self-focused scrutiny. Twentieth-century

---

[22] I can't help but stand on the soapbox and note that as I write this very morning, June 14, 2016, I read that the Supreme Court of the nation of Canada has officially abandoned the fear of the Lord by granting its physicians the power that the fictional spy James Bond was so famous for, namely, the "license to kill," a direct transgression of the Fifth Commandment (not to mention the old Hippocratic Oath: "I will use treatment to help the sick according to my ability and judgment, but never with a view to injury and wrongdoing. Neither will I administer a poison to anybody when asked to do so, nor will I suggest such a course.")

spiritual writer Bernard J. Kelly, C.S.Sp.[23] observed that "scrupulous people are the victims of a false concept of law which they obey under the compulsion of fear."[24] They perceive God as a tyrant and take no account of His mercy and kindness. "They want to make their future salvation a certainty even now through their own efforts; He wishes them to be saved by His mercy and nothing else. They fret and agitate themselves, are always in action, for fear gives them no rest: He wishes them to surrender themselves fully into His hands, to leave their salvation to His Omnipotence."[25]

As I write in this Jubilee Year of Mercy (and in the 800th Jubilee Year of the Dominican Order as well), I think of St. Catherine of Siena's powerful lines in her *Dialogue* when God told her that what troubled Him more than Judas's betrayal of His Son, Jesus Christ, was Judas's *despair* in that it deprecated the loving power of God's mercy and forgiveness. If God's forgiveness was there for the asking even for Christ's betrayer, why should we be so scrupulous as to doubt God's capacity to forgive us our sins? Why shouldn't our fear be, rather, that of disappointing Him in His superabundant mercy as the fount of all goodness and love for us?

THE POWER OF PRAYER TO FORGE FEAR AND FIRE OUR FURNACES OF LOVE

Those who fear God and love Him lift up their hearts and minds to Him in prayer. Indeed, St. Paul has advised us to "pray

---

[23] C.S.Sp. stands for Congregation of the Holy Ghost under the protection of the Immaculate Heart of Mary.

[24] Bernard J. Kelly, C.S.Sp., *The Seven Gifts* (New York: Sheed and Ward, 1942), p. 96.

[25] Ibid., pp. 97–98.

constantly" (1 Thess. 5:17). When we pray to God, we petition Him, asking for good things, and asking Him to spare us from evil. We thank Him for all the good things He showers us with, indeed, even the fact that He breathed life into us and sustains us in our existence. Our prayer shows proper fear of the Lord when our petitions for good things for ourselves keeps God's will and plans for us in mind, since He knows so much better than we do what we really need. Prayer is not a useless thing, though, since part of God's plan and explicit advice is that we talk to Him and ask Him for good things. Loving filial fear is also expressed in our prayer when we ask that God grant us the grace to act in ways that will please and not offend Him.

All manner of formal and informal prayers to God help dispose our souls to all manner of His graces. Although all Catholic prayers invoke the Holy Trinity either explicitly or implicitly, over the centuries, the spiritual treasure house of the Church has also amassed a bountiful store of prayers specifically directed to the Holy Spirit. As we progress through the gifts one by one, in the portions of our chapters devoted to prayer I'll present a small sample or two that we might pray as we read, asking the Holy Spirit to bless us with each gift. The opening quotation from the prologue provides the prayer as provided in the *Catechism of the Catholic Church*, no. 2671, drawing the first line from the Roman Missal Pentecost Service and the remaining lines from the Byzantine Liturgy, Pentecost Vespers, Troparion. Recall that first line, "Come, Holy Spirit, fill the hearts of your faithful *and enkindle in them the fire of your love*" (italics added). So now perhaps you see what inspired this section's heading.

The Holy Spirit came down upon Mary and the disciples on Pentecost in tongues of flame that gave them the gift of speaking in other tongues. Although you or I may or may not receive the charism of the gift of tongues in our day, the sanctifying gifts are for all of us, and having asked the Holy Spirit to come, we can also specifically ask Him to bless us with each and every one of the those seven gifts. Indeed, there are also Catholic prayers that ask for each gift by name. It seems quite fitting, then, to conclude this section on prayer for the gift of fear, with, well, a prayer for the gift of fear, this one from the great Church Doctor St. Alphonsus Liguori (1696–1787):

> O Giver of all supernatural gifts, who filled the soul of the Blessed Virgin Mary, Mother of God, with such immense favors, I beg You to visit me with Your grace and Your love and to grant me the gift of holy fear, so that it may act on me as a check to prevent me from falling back into my past sins, for which I beg pardon.[26]

HOW THE GIFT OF FEAR WATERS THE ROOTS OF HUMILITY AND TEMPERANCE AND FLOWS FROM THE VIRTUE OF HOPE

When St. Thomas wrote about the gifts in the *Summa Theologica*, he did so in the order of and the context of the theological virtues from which they flow or the cardinal virtues that they perfect. He addressed the gift of fear of the Lord when examining the virtue of *hope*. Being a supernatural virtue, the habit of hope is infused in us only through God's grace, and ultimately what we hope for is *to attain union with God in heaven by means of His divine assistance.*

---

[26] "Prayer for the Gifts of the Holy Spirit," posted at Catholic Online, http://www.catholic.org/prayers/prayer.php?p=773.

So where does the gift of fear fit in? Thomas notes that "God is the object of hope and fear, but under different aspects."[27] As hope has two objects—(1) the future good of heaven and (2) God's help to achieve it—fear also has two objects—(1) the evil of punishment and (2) God, from whom such punishment may come. The evil of God's punishment is only a relative evil, though, because from God flows only good. It is an evil that may befall us due to our own fault when we fail to fear God and follow the guidelines and aids He provides for our salvation.

So then, if we hope to spend eternity with God, the Holy Spirit's gift of fear is itself an invaluable aid, boosting us up the first rung of the ladder to heaven by helping us to reject the thoughts and behaviors that separate us from God when we do not take His power and His justice seriously. In this way it is a powerful counter to the sin of *presumption*, that perversion of hope that expects God to welcome us into heaven with no need for us to cooperate by trying to walk in the right upward direction in our thoughts, words, and deeds.

Now, recall from our opening quotation how St. Bonaventure compared the fear of the Lord to a beautiful tree watered by God, that when full grown is worthy of eternal life. When the virtue of hope is infused in our souls and the gift of fear is freely accepted, that fear takes root, and as the tree begins to grow tall, it branches out into a variety of other virtues, beatitudes, and fruits, such as these:

- *Humility*: John of St. Thomas has explained that humility is not the same thing as fear, because we may humble ourselves before those we do not fear, as Christ did when He washed the feet of His disciples, and yet, "humility

[27] *ST*, II-II, Q. 19, art. 1.

can flow from fear and be regulated by it."[28] He explains that St. Thomas noted that humility can be an effect of fear because anyone who perfectly fears God will not exalt himself in pride but will express the humility that recognizes our nothingness without God, who creates and sustains us. This calls to mind God's words to St. Catherine of Siena: "Do you know, daughter, who you are, and who I am? If you know these two things you will be blessed. You are she who is not; whereas I am He who is."[29]

- *Temperance*: The gift of fear also works to bring acts motivated by the virtue of temperance to a far higher perfection. Through temperance, we regulate our desires for pleasure and flee from sinful behaviors to avoid personal shame and to preserve our integrity, while the gift of fear works to repress our passions and our focus upon their delights, not to preserve our health or reputation, but out of reverence for God.

- *Poverty of Spirit*: St. Augustine observed and St. Thomas concurred that from the fear of the Lord flow both the virtue of humility and the beatitude of poverty of spirit. Per Augustine: "The fear of the Lord is befitting the humble of whom it is said: Blessed are the poor in spirit."[30] The fear of the Lord prompts not only the humility by which man avoids exalting himself before God, but also the

---

[28] John of St. Thomas, *The Gifts of the Holy Ghost* (New York: Sheed and Ward, 1951), p. 208.

[29] Blessed Raymond of Capua, *The Life of Saint Catherine of Siena* (Charlotte, NC: Saint Benedict Press, 2006), p. 54. See Exod. 3:14.

[30] *ST*, II-II, Q. 19, art. 12.

poverty of spirit through which man places God before all temporal goods, earthly treasures, and victories over others. As stated so well in Psalm 20:7: "Some boast of chariots, and some of horses; but we boast of the name of the LORD our God."[31]

♦ *Modesty, continency (self-control), and chastity*: Thomas notes that these are fruits of the Holy Spirit that correspond to the gift of fear, since they pertain to the moderate use of or abstention from temporal things or earthly goods and pleasures that may offend God.

So, how do we build these related virtues and enjoy the blessing of poverty of spirit, and the fruits that bring our passions under control? Well, we do nothing to *earn* the gift of fear, for it is *freely given*, but once we have received and unwrapped it, there are things that we must *do*, as Sts. Bonaventure and Paul have laid out so clearly for us (in a way that so appeals to the weightlifter in me):

Those who wish to have strong arms must give themselves to hard work. In a similar way, those who wish to have grace that strengthens them must give themselves to the practice of the virtues. The Apostle states: "By the grace of God I am what I am," and then adds, "I have labored more than all others."[32]

---

[31] If you will forgive the digression, I can't help but note my favorite ancient application of this particular verse. The ancient lives of St. Patrick of Ireland say that when warned by his Druid priests of St. Patrick's arrival and how it boded so poorly for the fate of their pagan religion, King O'Leary set forth "thrice-nine" chariots to intimidate the saint, whereupon Patrick, a man so immersed in the Scriptures, recited aloud this verse from memory!

[32] *Collations*, p. 36. See 1 Cor. 15:10.

THE BLESSED MOTHER SHOWS US HOW TO FEAR

If we are to learn to embrace fully the gifts of the Holy Spirit, what greater human example is there for us than the Blessed Virgin Mary, espoused of the Holy Spirit, made Mother of our Lord Jesus Christ, and given to us by Christ to be our Mother as well? St. Albert the Great (ca. 1200–1280), St. Thomas Aquinas's great teacher, wrote that when the angel Gabriel addressed Mary as "full of grace" (Luke 1:28) he essentially gave her a new name, a name that no other creature in the universe could claim. Mary was preserved from sin through her Immaculate Conception and was the open channel for all of God's graces, becoming literally "full of grace." Her response to Gabriel, "Let it be to me according to your word" (Luke 1:38), also served to open the founts of grace for us, through the birth, life, death, and Resurrection of her Son, Jesus Christ.

St. Albert notes in his book *Mariale* that to say that Mary was "full of grace" means that she was gifted with *all* of the virtues and graces, including the intellectual, cardinal, and theological virtues, the seven gifts of the Holy Spirit, the eight beatitudes, and the twelve fruits of the Holy Spirit. Indeed, he provides as well a fascinating look at Blessed Mary as she was prefigured in Isaiah 11:1: "There shall come forth a shoot from the stump of Jesse, and a branch shall grow out of his roots." This shoot, notes St. Albert, represents Mary as Mother of God. The shoots are "long and straight, upright and solid, graceful and flexible—here are all the symbols of the graces of Mary."[33] The branch, of course,

---

[33] Cited in Rev. Robert J. Bushmiller, *The Maternity of Mary in the Mariology of St. Albert the Great* (dissertation, University of Fribourg, Switzerland, 1959), p. 30.

is Christ, who, in the very next verse (indeed, the foundational verse of this book), is rested upon by the Holy Spirit, receiving all seven gifts. St. Albert notes as well in his *Commentary on St. Luke* that "the virginal process in which the stalk gives birth to the flower recalls the virginal birth."[34]

Mary, then, has received all the graces and cooperates in bringing us Christ and His New Law, letting loose those graces of the Holy Spirit for us all. No wonder one of the Blessed Mother's many titles is Mediatrix of All Graces, operating not through her own power, but through the power of her Son, having been given this role, although a creature, as a free gift from God for her complete cooperation in God's plan for our redemption.[35]

So, what can Mary teach us about the fear of the Lord? Good question. Although Mary was without sin, she clearly displayed the heights of a loving filial fear in her question to Gabriel after he told her she would bear the "Son of the Most High": "How can this be, since I have no husband?" (Luke 1:34). Mary's question shows that she surely knew how babies usually came into the world! Still, the fact that she was already betrothed to Joseph reveals she had previously made a vow of perpetual virginity. She showed fear of the Lord then, lest the angel was suggesting that she would break her vow.

Mothers teach us by their words, but even more so by their examples. In 1874, Reverend Henry Formby, O.S.D.,[36] published

---

[34] Ibid.

[35] For an easily accessible modern summary of the history and meaning of this title, see Fr. William C. Most's "Mary, Mediatrix of All Graces" at https://www.ewtn.com/faith/teachings/marya4. htm.

[36] Third Order of St. Dominic.

a book nobly entitled, *Sacrum Septenarium, or The Seven Gifts of the Holy Ghost as Exemplified in the Life and Person of the Blessed Virgin for the Guidance and Instruction of Her Children*, in which he focused specifically on how Mary can help us grow in the gifts, as any loving mother would want us to do. I drew from that tome the lesson of Mary's vow and how it relates to the gift of fear. Fortunately for us, Father Formby formulated Marian lessons on each one of the gifts, and we'll gratefully pull from them in the chapters ahead.

Now, though, we will turn to the lessons of the branch who, as Isaiah foretold, would grow from the shoot that was Mary and would receive and employ most perfectly all of the *sacrum septenarium*, "seven gifts."

THE FEAR OF THE LORD IN THE LORD JESUS CHRIST

We said earlier that Christ received the seven gifts, but could He have fear of the Lord when He *is* the Lord? Sounds as if I have some 'splainin' to do! Fortunately, I can draw from St. Thomas and others. Jesus Christ, of course, is the Word of God, the second person of the Trinity incarnate and made man. Jesus Christ had both divine and human intellects and wills, divine power along with potential human limitations, but He always kept them aligned. He did not sin and was God, so He would have had no servile fear dreading punishment, yet He had complete reverence for the Father and sought only to do the Father's will. Indeed, He declared, "I and the Father are one" (John 10:30). Facing the pains of Crucifixion while in human flesh, Jesus famously prayed "Father, if thou art willing, remove this cup from me," and yet He also added, "nevertheless not my will, but thine, be done" (Luke 22:42; cf. Matt. 26:39).

Jesus so loved God the Father that He embraced the Holy Spirit's gift of filial fear to prevail over any fear of unimaginable sufferings that He would feel in His flesh for the sake of each and every one of us. Although there have been and probably will continue to be martyrs for Christ, who among us will likely ever have to face willingly a horror like Christ's Passion on the Cross? Can we then thank the Holy Spirit for the great gift of fear that can help us reject whatever attachment we have to things of this earth that might bar our way to heaven?

PROFILE IN GIFTEDNESS #1

FROM SAUL TO ST. PAUL
WITH FEAR AND TREMBLING

Saul of Tarsus was a merciless persecutor of the Christians. Indeed, as the deacon Stephen, the first martyr for Christ, was stoned to death and cried out, asking that the Lord not hold the sin against the mob who stoned him, young Saul was right there "consenting to his death" (Acts 8:1). Of course, a funny thing happened to Saul soon after on the road to Damascus, where he had planned to gather more Christians for persecution in Jerusalem. He was blinded by a flash of light, fell to the ground, and heard a voice asking, "Saul, Saul, why do you persecute me?" When Saul asked who had spoken, the voice responded "I am Jesus, whom you are persecuting" (Acts 9:4–5). Saul, still blind, was carried into Damascus, and God told the disciple Ananias that Saul was His chosen instrument to carry His message to the Gentiles and the Israelites. Ananias went to Saul and told him, "The Lord Jesus ... has sent me that you may regain your sight and be filled with the Holy Spirit" (Acts 9:17). Ananias laid his hands on Saul, scales fell from Saul's eyes, and his sight returned.

After Saul was filled with the Holy Spirit and His gifts, he immediately began proclaiming in the synagogues that Jesus was the Son of God. Later, as the carrier of Christ's message to the Gentiles, he no longer used his Hebrew name of Saul, but went by his Latin name, Paul, to accommodate his potential non-Jewish converts throughout the Roman Empire, of which he was a citizen.

Paul's conversion to Christ was a swift and powerful transformation through the power of the Holy Spirit, but Paul cooperated with that awesome gift of grace for the rest of his life — indeed, in "fear and trembling" (1 Cor. 2:3; cf. Phil. 2:12). His filial fear of the Lord was palpable. He sought only to live through and as Christ, and to bring the world to Christ as well, so deep was his fear of offending Him whom He loved. His filial fear set him free from any presumption that heaven was guaranteed him because of the great graces God gave him. He advised the Christians of Corinth to practice unremitting self-control in subduing their bodies, explaining that he must do the same "lest after preaching to others I myself should be disqualified" (1 Cor. 9:27).

St. Paul, the Apostle to the Gentiles, shares a feast day with St. Peter, the rock on which Christ built the Church, on June 29.

> St. Paul, pray for us, that we too may work out
> our salvation with the filial fear of the Lord,
> and inspire our neighbors to do the same.

ANGELIC ANAYLSIS #1

THE GIFTS IN SACRED SCRIPTURE

So where in the Bible are the seven gifts of the Holy Spirit? Scripture itself was inspired by the Source of the seven gifts, and their Source Himself appears in Scripture's very first verses: "In the beginning God created the heavens and the earth. The earth was without form and void, and darkness was upon the face of the deep; and the Spirit of God was moving over the face of the waters" (Gen. 1:1–2). God's Holy Spirit is the Giver of these life-giving gifts as He moves over the waters to breathe within the depths of our own innermost beings.

Most of the *gifts* and their related *virtues* share the same names. In fact, one task we will face, as St. Thomas did, will be to distinguish the two kinds of special blessings and perfections that we receive from God in different ways. While the gifts appear alone or grouped together in hundreds of places throughout the Bible, there is one essential place in which all are listed together:

> There shall come forth a shoot from the stump of Jesse,
>> and a branch shall grow out of his roots.
> And the Spirit of the LORD shall rest upon him,
>> the spirit of wisdom and understanding,
>> the spirit of counsel and might,
>> the spirit of knowledge and the fear of the LORD.
> And his delight shall be in the fear of the LORD. (Isa. 11:1–3)

Latin Vulgate translation courtesy of St. Jerome:

Et egredietur virga de radice Jesse, et flos de radice ejus ascendet. Et requiescet super eum spiritus Domini: spiritus sapientiae et intellectus, spiritus consilii et fortitudinis, spiritus scientiae et *pietatis*; et replebit eum spiritus timoris Domini. (Italics added)

In the Douay-Rheims edition of the Bible, translated from the Latin, we find the word *godliness* meaning essentially the same thing as *piety*. Although some translations of the Bible show fear of the Lord a second time instead of piety, St. Jerome used the word *pietatas* (piety) for the spirit following *scientiae* (science or knowledge) and used *timoris Domini* (fear of the Lord) at the end of verse 3. The name of the gift of piety has hence come down through Tradition from the early Church Fathers to Pope St. Gregory the Great, to St. Thomas Aquinas, and is listed among the gifts in our current *Catechism of the Catholic Church* (no. 1831).

PROFILE IN GRACE #1

ST. JEROME AND THE GIFT OF THE LATIN VULGATE BIBLE

There are some gifts of the Holy Spirit that we can hold in our hands, and one was handed to the Church by Eusebius Sophronius Hieronymus—better known as St. Jerome (347–420). Jerome was one of the four original Latin Doctors of the Church (along with Sts. Ambrose, Augustine, and Pope Gregory the Great) and is known as the Father of Biblical Science. His greatest gift to us was the Latin Vulgate Bible, an elegant and faithful translation from Hebrew and Greek sources into the *vulgar*, or common, Latin used by the people in his day, rendering the Bible more understandable and engaging than ever before for a Latin-reading audience. It influenced theologians for centuries and in the sixteenth century was promulgated at the Council of Trent as the authentic Latin translation for use by the Church.

Jerome as a man and a saint shows how God showers His gifts on all kinds of people with all kinds of personalities, sometimes producing from surly sinners some startling saintly surprises! In his youth Jerome was engrossed in sensual pleasures and so immersed in classical pagan philosophy and literature that even decades after his conversion he was flogged by an angel in a dream for being more Ciceronian than Christian![37] As a mature hermit, in his tireless efforts to defend the Church, Jerome sometimes wrote

---

[37] See Profile in Grace #4 for a brief look at Cicero and his influence on many Christian theologians.

very harshly about his theological opponents and was prone to arguments and estrangements from his family and friends. He is the patron saint of translators, librarians, and encyclopedists and could be patron of the hot-tempered too!

Still, he was also known for his penitence and his attempts at reconciliation with some of his foes. Centuries after Jerome's death, Pope Sixtus V (1521–1590) saw a painting depicting Jerome beating his breast as the tax collector in Luke 18:13 did (and as we do at Mass in the Penitential Rite), but Jerome was holding a stone. The pope said to the figure of St. Jerome in the painting that if it were not for the pebble he held, he would not be a saint!

St. Jerome has special relevance for us in our consideration of the seven gifts of the Holy Spirit, because his rendering of the names of the gifts in the Vulgate has formed the basis of sixteen hundred years of deeper reflection on the gifts within Church Tradition. And why did St. Jerome consider the study of Scripture so important that he would spend years learning Greek and Hebrew and would sequester himself in a cave outside Bethlehem, laboring every day for years on end to bring to the world the Vulgate? Thankfully, he told us exactly why in his *Commentary on Isaiah*: "Ignorance of the Scriptures is ignorance of Christ."

St. Jerome's feast day is September 30.

St. Jerome, Father of Biblical Science, pray for us, so that under the guidance of the Holy Spirit we may grow in our knowledge of and love for Christ as we read Scripture.

CHAPTER 2

PRACTICING PIETY

St. Thomas remarks that the gift of piety
looks upon God as a Father.

—John of St. Thomas, *The Gifts of the Holy Ghost*

Piety then, in the sense of a gift of the Holy Ghost,
is a power given us of submitting ourselves to the
Holy Ghost breathing into our souls a spirit of
childlike reverence for Our Heavenly Father and
of devotion to the furthering of His interests.

—Bernard J. Kelly, C.S.Sp., *The Seven Gifts*

DO YOU HONOR YOUR FATHER AND MOTHER (AND SISTERS AND BROTHERS) WITH PIETY?

We saw on our first step up the spiritual ladder that the gift of fear is perfected in us as the punishment-dreading fear that is found in a servant (*servile fear*) is replaced by the fear of failure to disappoint a parent, as is found in a loving son or daughter (*filial fear*). We may now ask St. Thomas to begin to help us unwrap this second sacred gift, known by the name of *piety*.

THE ESSENCE, EXERCISE, AND ORIGINS OF PIETY

To those who would argue that piety is not a gift of the Holy Spirit, but merely a virtue, Thomas notes that gifts are habitual dispositions that make us open to the stirrings of the Holy Spirit, and one of the ways that the Spirit moves us is toward a "filial affection towards God," here citing Romans 8:15: "You have received the spirit of sonship. When we cry, 'Abba! Father!'"[38]

The natural virtue of piety, as philosophers such as Cicero have pointed out, entails providing service and honor to our

---

[38] To avoid burdening you with a superabundance of footnotes, please note that all quotations from St. Thomas in this section come from *ST*, II-II, Q. 121, and all quotations from St. Bonaventure come from his collation on the gift of piety.

parents and to our country, whereas the *gift* of piety entails primarily that we honor and serve God *as Father*, and secondarily, that we honor and serve, because of their relationship to God, our parents, neighbors (being brothers and sisters in Christ), the entire Communion of Saints—and even Scripture, as piety, according to St. Augustine, guides us not to contradict Scripture. John of St. Thomas elucidates that the gift of piety reveres God not only as Father but also as the principle of all *graces*, which He pours out on us as His adopted sons and daughters. The gift of piety then, is truly a family affair!

Speaking of family and the great Communion of Saints, we'll next take a quick look at the gift of piety through a couple of addition lenses (bifocals, we might say) to perfect our spiritual vision, provided most aptly by St. Bonaventure, the "Seraphic Doctor."[39] In his Lenten collation on the gift of piety, Bonaventure dealt us another pair of threes to elucidate a gift of the Holy Spirit, this time three exercises of the gift of piety and then the origins thereof.

Recall that some Bibles, including the Douay-Rheims, translate the gift in Isaiah 11:2 as "godliness" rather than "piety." In his examination of piety, St. Bonaventure begins by citing St. Paul

---

[39] Doctors of the Catholic Church have traditionally been given one or more titles to honor and distinguish them. St. Thomas Aquinas, for example, being known as the Common Doctor and the Angelic Doctor, St. Jerome is called the Biblical Doctor, and St. Augustine is called the Doctor of Grace. St. Bonaventure is known as the Seraphic Doctor because of his great love for God. The seraphim are considered in Catholic tradition the highest class of angels, those who see God most clearly as they circle about his throne, singing, "Holy, holy, holy ..." (as in the Sanctus of the Mass; see Isa. 6:3; Rev. 4:8).

in 1 Timothy 4:7: "Train yourself in piety."[40] This is Bonaventure's springboard to exhort us to train ourselves in the exercise of piety after we have accepted it as a gift from the Holy Spirit. "The exercise of piety consists of three acts; namely, the reverence of divine worship, the guarding of interior holiness, and the superabundance of interior compassion." Here's a brief summary of his three ways, all of which are buttressed by plenty of scriptural references and citations, of which I'll provide just a few. (And I'll provide the *italics* for emphasis.) Let's see if they can inspire us to exercise these pious acts in our souls.

THREE WAYS PIETY IS EXERCISED PER THE SERAPHIC DOCTOR

1. *Reverence of divine worship.* St. Bonaventure begins by citing Sirach 49:3–4, which refers to the way Josiah, King of Judah, turned away from abominations and impiety and turned his heart to the Lord. St. Bonaventure notes that, before Christ, the worship of God flourished only among the Israelites, but even then not at all times. Pious worship reached its heights with David and reached the depths of impious idolatry with Manasseh, until Josiah came to power and strengthened piety through the proper worship of God. He notes as well that Augustine said that the Greek word *theosebia*, "piety," also means the worship of God. We exercise our piety muscles, then, when we turn our hearts and minds away from false gods and reverently worship only God.

2. *Guarding of interior holiness.* St. Bonaventure notes that in 1 Timothy 2:1 we are called to pray and make

---

[40] This appears as "Train yourself in godliness" in the RSV.

supplication for all men, so that, as verse 2 makes clear, "we may lead a quiet ... life in all piety and chastity." Bonaventure expounds that we "must understand that the Christian religion is summed up in piety and purity. No one can have an attitude of piety toward himself without possessing peace. This is the Christian religion, which consists in two things. The tranquility of peace is found only in the tranquility of conscience. And conscience is not holy unless it is good and pious; that is, unless it prefers a life of virtue and grace to the life of nature." (Recall that Bonaventure gave the *cleansing of conscience* as the first perfection of the gift of fear. Each gift disposes us to the grace that is regulated and perfected by yet higher gifts.)

3. *Abundance of internal compassion.* St. Bonaventure starts with an explication of Sirach 44:10–11, in which it is reported that people of mercy whose pious deeds have not failed will bring prosperity to their offspring and to their children's children. Citing examples of Noah, Abraham, Moses, Joseph, and Samuel, St. Bonaventure explains that if we are to exercise piety toward God as Father, we too must act as holy fathers to those who come after us. (Now, is that not an intriguing insight? To exercise the gift of piety, we need to "pay it forward," as they say today, to those who depend on us.)

THREE ORIGINS OF THE GIFT OF PIETY PER THE SERAPHIC DOCTOR

1. *God the Father.* We know from the book of Genesis that we are made in the image of God. When we are pious toward God as our Father, we become like Him

when we behave like a merciful father. Sirach 2:11 tells us that God is compassionate and merciful, forgiving sins, and Psalm 103:13 tells us that God pities those who fear Him as a father pities his children. We might ask ourselves, as St. Bonaventure asks us: "Since the glorious God has compassion on the suffering, why do you not imitate God? If there were a fountain of water that could enable dried plants to become green again, it would be greatly appreciated. The river of divine mercy flows in great abundance and makes dead plants green again. Should you not bring that stream into your soul? But you cannot bring it in if you do not have piety."

2. *The incarnate Wisdom.* Expounding on 1 Timothy 2:14, Bonaventure notes that the great mystery of our religion is the holocaust through which Christ offered Himself on the Cross for us, for which He gave us the sacrament of the altar so that, "being mindful of the sacrament of piety, we might put on the heart of piety.[41] 'Cruel is the heart that is not softened by this.'"

3. *Holy Mother Church sanctified by the Holy Spirit.* "The Holy Spirit makes us to be children of one father and one mother, and members of one body." Bonaventure notes that Psalm 133:1–2 relates that when brothers dwell in unity it is "like oil on the head that runs down the beard, the beard of Aaron." The "oil of piety," he elaborates, is first on the head and then trickles down to all parts of the body. The pope and the bishops

---

[41] See Colossians 3:12: "Put on ... a heart of mercy."

especially, then, must generously share that pious oil "that must be possessed by all."

SACRAMENTAL SOURCES OF PIETY

Christ promised to send us the Paraclete, and He initiated the seven sacraments to bring that Holy Spirit's graces into our souls, initially through Baptism, and then strengthened through Confirmation. All of the sacraments, in fact, can help us grow in the gift of piety. St. Bonaventure, as we saw, called the Eucharist "the sacrament of piety," and an essential part of the Eucharistic prayer is the *epiclesis*, from the Greek for "invocation," or "calling down from on high," in which the Holy Spirit is asked to bless the bread and wine that will become Christ in the institution narrative. So, the next time you are at Mass, be alert to the action and presence of the Holy Spirit in Christ's "sacrament of piety."

When St. Bonaventure talks of the "oil of piety," we can hark back to its scriptural foundation and associations with the Holy Spirit—for example, when Jesus echoed Isaiah 61:1 and said: "The Spirit of the Lord is upon me, because he has anointed me" (Luke 4:18). We can also see how the "oil of piety," signifying the working of the Holy Spirit, is used in Baptism, Confirmation, the Anointing of the Sick (see James 5:14), and Holy Orders. Oil is also used in the consecration of new churches. Those who receive the oil in Holy Orders, especially the pope and bishops, are responsible for dispersing that oil of piety to the laity, and the laity should willingly soak it up, being cleansed and strengthened by it. Even the sacrament of Matrimony, although oil is not used in the rite, can strengthen us in piety, as it marks the transformation of men and women into the earthly fathers and mothers of the next generation of sons and daughters of Christ.

PIETY'S PREVENTATIVES

Clearly, then, it is no small thing to follow the Holy Spirit's
prompting to honor God as our Father and our neighbors as brothers and sisters. But in what ways might we prevent the flow of
that "oil of piety"? We might ask ourselves questions like these:

- Do I focus too much on God as a Master or Judge? Do
  I tend to think of God foremost as an abstract force or
  power, as the First Cause, as the Unmoved Mover, as
  merely the God of the reasoning philosophers, question-
  ing whether He really has any personal interest in me
  or in any person?[42] Do I think much about God at all?
  If we answer yes to the first two questions or no to the
  second, we have not paid due attention to the adoptive
  sonship that Christ has earned for us, so that we too may
  call God *Abba* (Father).[43]

- Have I succumbed to the green-eyed monster of *envy*?
  When we envy our neighbors, feeling sad when good
  things come their way, we act contrary to the gift of

---

[42] Know that after St. Thomas Aquinas proves, with the philosophers and St. Paul (see Rom. 1:19–20), that reason can indeed
demonstrate that God is the First Cause, the Unmoved Mover,
and the Necessary Being, the Source and Sustainer of all that
exists, he moves further through faith, recalling that God Himself told Moses as much when Moses asked God His name, in a
response we can translate in as few as two words: "I AM" (Exod.
3:14). The god of the philosophers is indeed as well "the God of
Abraham, the God of Isaac, and the God of Jacob" (Exod. 3:15).
And this one true God is also a Father indeed, as we learned
from his coeternal Son and Word Incarnate, "before Abraham
was, I am" (John 8:58).

[43] Some translators note that the term is close to the English word
"Daddy," implying an intimate, affectionate closeness.

piety. We do not recognize that others are our brothers and sisters in Christ, children of the same Father, who wants good things for us all and wants us to want good things for each other!

- Have I become so self-absorbed in seeking my own "*personal* relationship with Jesus Christ" that I have become indifferent to others, forgetting my call to call my neighbor to join in the family of our mother Church, that third source, per Bonaventure, from which the gift of piety flows?

PIOUS PRAYER

When Cardinal Maria Martini (1927–2012) preached a series of spiritual exercises for the Diocese of Milan in the 1990s, the first gift he spoke on was piety, and his first words on piety stressed its relation to prayer. "It is this gift that gives us a taste for prayer and makes us pray willingly and with enthusiasm; it makes a prayer come from our heart that is fluid, serene and calm."[44] Indeed, when His disciples asked Him how to pray, Christ's first words of prayer were, of course, "Our Father." As the two words "I AM" dramatically declare the truth of God the All-Powerful Creator, so too do the two words "Our Father" express the breathtaking truth that the All-Powerful is also the All-Loving and has offered us eternal membership in His family. Strictly speaking, the gift of piety offers God honor and glory as our Father, and what well-known prayer more tersely sums it up than the Glory Be? "Glory be to the Father, and to the Son, and to the Holy

---

[44] Cardinal Maria Martini and Dom Guéranger, *The Gifts of the Holy Spirit* (London: St. Paul's Publishing, 1998), p. 23.

Spirit, as it was in the beginning, is now, and ever shall be, world without end. Amen."

Turning again to the prayer of St. Alphonsus Liguori, we conclude this section by asking the Holy Spirit to shower us with this gift: "Grant me the gift of piety, so that I may serve You for the future with increased fervor, follow with more promptness Your holy inspirations, and observe your divine precepts with greater fidelity."

PIETY PERFECTS VARIOUS VIRTUES

Piety, like all of the other gifts except fear of the Lord, shares its name with a virtue. St. Thomas examined the gift of piety after he examined the virtue, and he did so in the context of 55 questions, hundreds of articles, and indeed, in the edition I use, 173 pages (in double-column print) examining the cardinal virtue of justice from virtually every conceivable angle! If we build these virtuous habits within our souls, we can perfect them with the assistance of the Holy Spirit's gifts. Let's take just the briefest of whirlwind tours here to see what kinds of virtues and virtuous behaviors are related to and perfected by the gift of fear.

The gift of piety helps to perfect the cardinal virtue of *justice*. In justice we give to others their rightful due in equal measure, but God has given us so much—our very existence and every good that we have—that we can never full repay Him! John of St. Thomas explains that the gift of piety transcends the idea of benefits and debts, honoring and magnifying God for His own sake, as the Psalmist declares, "O magnify the Lord with me, and let us extol his name together."[45]

---

[45] Ps. 34:3, as cited in *The Gifts*, p. 180.

As for the beatitudes, St. Thomas mentions that although the subject matter and behaviors of the fourth and fifth beatitudes, "Blessed are they that *hunger and thirst after righteousness*," and "Blessed are the *merciful*," do indeed correspond to piety, St. Augustine noted a connection to *meekness* as well. St. Thomas explains that *meekness*, which controls the emotion of anger, removes impediments to acts of piety.

Finally, as for the fruits, Thomas declares that *goodness*, and *benignity* flow from the gift of piety, and *mildness*, which controls the acts of our anger, also removes obstacles to pious acts.

MOTHER MARY HELPS US MAGNIFY THE LORD

Recall how John of St. Thomas cited the psalmist's call to "magnify the Lord" and "extol his name" in exercise of piety. Who is so famous for the way she magnified the Lord that an entire prayer called the Magnificat uses her words recorded in Luke 1:46–55? The Blessed Mother Mary, of course, and her prayer starts with the unforgettable words, "My soul magnifies the Lord."

Mother Mary does well for us what mothers are supposed to do in guiding us toward heaven by their words and deeds. She so clearly honored and magnified God from the days of her youth when she consented to the power of the Holy Spirit to conceive in her the very Son of God who would call us to be His brothers. When her Son had become a man, her piety would prompt Him to perform His first recorded miracle.

At the wedding feast in Cana, Mary sensed the distress and shame the young married couple would feel if they failed in hospitality to their guests by running out of wine. So she sought out her Son and simply said, "They have no wine." After Jesus declared, "My hour has not yet come," Mary still told the servants,

"Do whatever he tells you" (John 1:2–5). Thereupon, He whose sacramental blood would one day take the place of wine, turned water into wine for the guests. Mary's pious compassion was as evident as her advice to the servants was wise. Indeed, that advice is forever applicable to each and every one of her children, even to this day: "Do whatever he tells you."

Just a few years later, Mary would heed her own advice as she trusted in the wisdom of her Son even when it led to His death on the Cross in front of her own weeping eyes. She knew that the Father's will was always to be done. Her pain would turn to joy three days later when Jesus rose from His tomb, and fifty days after that the Holy Spirit once again came to her in a most dramatic way, as she was in that room with the disciples when He descended upon them in tongues of holy fire (Acts 2:1–4).

Mary presents for us the ultimate fully human model of the gift of piety toward our heavenly Father, but we should pay close attention as well to the Holy Spirit's promptings to show *piety toward Mary*, not as God, but as His masterpiece of creation. In his writings on the gifts, Father Bernard Joseph Kelly noted that the saints are particularly dear to God, as we see by the great gifts of grace with which He supplied them. Therefore, to admire and honor the saints is to

> praise the works of Our Father Himself.... And what we have said of the saints is a thousand times more true if applied to Our Blessed Lady.... To be lacking in devotion to Mary is to fail in piety to God. To refuse to be devout to her as a child should be to its mother is again to be lacking in piety to Him, because He made her to be our mother. Piety is a gift which, concentrating the soul on God its Father, makes it big enough and

warm enough to embrace all mankind and the angels and saints as well."[46]

CHRIST AND THE FATHER ARE ONE IN PERFECT PIETY

Piety is one of the gifts of the Holy Spirit that makes us amenable to His guidance on our journey toward lasting union with God, particularly through reverence for God as Father and all that that entails. Christ, of course, was one with the Father (see John 10:30), and He explicitly told us to think of and pray to God, "Our Father." He also said much more than that to instruct us in piety. We are to love God as children—humble, innocent, generous, and full of the desire to please our parents. Jesus said: "Truly, I say to you, unless you turn and become like children, you will never enter the kingdom of heaven. Whoever humbles himself like this child, he is the greatest in the kingdom of heaven" (Matt. 18:3–4). We saw that Pope St. Gregory the Great wrote that "through the fear of the Lord we rise to piety" and that close to the gift of fear of the Lord is the virtue of humility. Fear of the Lord, then, is like a rebirth, and piety represents a new childhood, one that we must never completely outgrow, following the example of Christ, who always sought to please His Father and bring salvation to us, whom He made His brothers and sisters despite the ultimate sacrifice involved.

[46] *The Seven Gifts*, p. 86.

PROFILE IN GIFTEDNESS #2

ST. THÉRÈSE OF LISIEUX AND THE LITTLE WAY OF PIETY

St. Thérèse of Lisieux (1873–1897) shows us how to love and honor God as Father in perfectly *childlike*, though not *childish* ways. Thérèse boldly sought Pope Leo XIII's permission, face-to-face, to enter the Carmelite Order at the young age of fifteen. The pope deferred to the judgment of her local superiors, and Thérèse soon received the consent of her bishop and the prioress. She entered the cloistered Carmelite monastery in Lisieux, France, on April 9, 1888, which because of the timing of Lent, would be Annunciation Day that year.

There, for the next nine years, behind the cloister walls, the pious teen would flower into one of our modern day's greatest saints and the third female Doctor of the Church, joining such giants as Sts. Augustine and Thomas Aquinas. Through her writings, including the autobiographical *Story of a Soul* and the writings and recollections of others who knew her well, including her biological sisters who were also sisters in Christ at the monastery with her, Thérèse has shown us how the heavenly Father has provided such graces to us all, that each of us, regardless of how insignificant our role in life may seem, may serve and love God in glorious ways

- by the very simplest of our pious thoughts, menial chores, small acts of kindness
- by our acts of patience when we are put upon by others
- by enduring whatever sufferings might come our way

In one of her prayers, Thérèse, known as the Little Flower, calls these simple things flowers that she "throws" to God: "Throwing flowers means offering You, as first fruits, the least sighs, the deepest woes, my joys and my sorrows, my little sacrifices."

Thérèse's way is childlike in that it bespeaks total trust in, honor toward, and love for God as a loving Father with Jesus as our Brother. Thérèse had a special affection for the Christ Child and took the name Thérèse of the Child Jesus, but her spirituality was also very mature. Early in her religious life, she was given permission to add "and of the Holy Face" to her religious title. This was a popular devotion at the time, and Thérèse was particularly taken by the image of Christ in His humanity and the great suffering He would endure as described in Isaiah 53:1–5 and 63:1–5.

As she honored God as Father and Christ as Brother, Thérèse also had the most pious devotion to the Blessed Virgin as Mother. She emphasized how Mary glorified God in the simplest acts of her daily life, being more a mother than a queen, and Thérèse provided the fascinating insight that, in one way, we are more fortunate than Mary was since she did not have a Blessed Virgin to love!

Thérèse can inspire us all to reach a higher state of piety, and this more modern saint has even provided a metaphor of spiritual growth that updates our spiritual ladder. Indeed, she declared that rather than climbing the mystical Mount Carmel, she needed to take God's elevator!

And what a fitting metaphor that is for spiritual growth through the gifts. We don't rise merely from our own efforts, but by allowing God to lift us as a father does a child.

St. Thérèse died before the age of twenty-five. She suffered many months from tuberculosis and had some dark nights of doubt and of pain. On the night of September 30, 1897, clutching a crucifix, she cried out, "Oh! I love Him!... My God ... I love you!" and her soul ascended to meet Him.

St. Thérèse's feast day is October 1.

St. Thérèse, pray for us, so that we, through our own little ways, may honor God as our Father, Mary as our Mother, Christ as our Brother, and the Communion of Saints and all of our neighbors as our brothers and sisters.

THE HOLY SPIRIT AS LOVE AND GIFT

I answer that, the name Love in God can be taken essentially
and personally. If taken personally it is the proper name of
the Holy Ghost: as Word is the proper name of the Son.

—St. Thomas Aquinas, *Summa Theologica*, I, Q. 37, art. 1

I answer that, Gift, taken personally in God, is
the proper name of the Holy Ghost.

—St. Thomas Aquinas, *Summa Theologica*, I, Q. 38, art. 2

The *Catechism of the Catholic Church* (no. 684) explains that
although the Holy Spirit was the last person of the Holy Trinity to be revealed to us, "through his grace, the Holy Spirit is
the first to awaken faith in us and to communicate to us the
new life," which is to "know the Father and the one whom he
has sent, Jesus Christ" (see John 17:3). We come to know the
Father and the Son through the stirrings of the Holy Spirit in
our soul.

The term *spirit* translates the Hebrew word *ruah*, which means
"breath," "air," or "wind." It comes to us from the Latin word
spiritus, and in English has typically been translated "spirit,"
although some translators, especially in days gone by, have also
used the synonym "ghost" to mean exactly the same thing. All
readers have certainly heard of the Holy Ghost, and this name
happens to be used in the translation of St. Thomas's *Summa
Theologica* by the Fathers of the English Dominican Province

that I routinely use, which is why it appears in this chapter's opening quotations.

Although Christ has instructed us to call this Third Person by the name "Holy Spirit," the Holy Spirit is also known by many other titles. Christ called Him the "Paraclete" or "Counselor" as well as "the Spirit of truth" (John 14:16). The *Catechism* (693) relates that in other books of the New Testament He is called the "Spirit of the promise," the "Spirit of adoption," the "Spirit of Christ," the "Spirit of the Lord," the "Spirit of God," and the "Spirit of glory."

In his masterful modern summary of the writings of Pope Saint John Paul II on the Holy Spirit, Fr. Bill McCarthy, MSA, has provided a full list of the fifty-two scriptural titles and images of the Holy Spirit, including Spirit of Love (Gal. 5:22) and Gift (John 3:34; Act 2:38; 10:45).[47]

St. Thomas Aquinas, like great teachers who came before him and since, has zoomed in on two names of the Holy Spirit especially suited for our examination of His seven *loving gifts*: *Love* and *Gift*.

LOVE WITH A CAPITAL *L*

St. Thomas tells us, following Pope St. Gregory the Great: "The Holy Ghost Himself is Love."[48] He elaborates further that the Holy Spirit is said to be the bond of Love between the Father

---

[47] Fr. Bill McCarthy, MSA, *The Holy Spirit in the Writings of Pope John Paul II* (McKees Rocks, PA: St. Andrew's Productions, 2001), 490–491.

[48] All quotations from St. Thomas within this paragraph are from his *Summa Theologica* (*ST*), Q. 37, art. 1.

and the Son and that "from the fact that the Father and the Son mutually love one another, it necessarily follows that this mutual Love, the Holy Ghost, proceeds from both. As regards origin, therefore, the Holy Ghost is not the medium, but the third person in the Trinity."

To make matters more amazing, more loving, and more beautiful, St. Thomas also expounds upon St. Augustine's profound declaration that the Father and the Son love each other by the Holy Spirit. St. Thomas explains that the phrase "to love" can be taken two ways. In one sense, it means that the Father and the Son love each other by Their own essence. In another, it means that the Father and the Son "spirate," or breathe, the love that is the Holy Spirit. Further, "the Father loves not only the Son, but also Himself and us, by the Holy Ghost."

Perhaps these thoughts are over our heads, but it is well worth it to try to wrap our heads around them (or, as we'll soon see when we examine the gifts of the Holy Spirit, to allow Love Himself to help us understand).

THE GIFT WHO KEEPS ON GIVING

Love is expressed in a fundamental way in the act of giving. After addressing Love as a name of the Holy Spirit, Thomas next considers His holy name of Gift, starting with a quotation from St. Augustine: "'As the body of flesh is nothing but flesh; so the gift of the Holy Ghost is nothing but the Holy Ghost.' But the Holy Ghost is a personal name; so also therefore is Gift."[49]

---

[49] *ST*, I, Q. 38, art. 1. All italics in quotations from the *Summa Theologica* throughout this book are in the original edition of the Fathers of the English Dominican Provinces (New York: Benziger

Thomas explicates that the word *gift* denotes a capacity for being given, "and what is given has an aptitude or relation both to the giver and to that to which is given. For it would not be given by anyone unless it was his to give; and it is given to someone to be his."[50] (After all, as some Scholastic theologians are wont to say, "You can't give what you don't have!") Thomas explains further that only a divine Person may give divine things, and of all creatures on earth, only human beings have been given by God the capacity to receive, enjoy, and use the divine gifts of the Holy Spirit. Only we have the capacity freely to know and love God rightly. Still, although we possess these receptive rational powers, we can receive these divine gifts and possess God only when He gives them and thereby gives Himself to us as a *gift*. In other words, the Holy Spirit, "Love proceeding," freely gives us the gift of Himself!

St. Thomas elaborates that the Holy Spirit gives us Himself as a free, gratuitous, nonreturnable gift of love, as we do when we give loving gifts to others with no expectation of personal gain, because we wish them well. Love itself, then, is the "first gift through which all free gifts are given. So since the Holy Ghost proceeds as love ... He proceeds as the first gift."[51] Further, as St. Augustine says in his book on the Trinity, "By the gift, which is the Holy Ghost, many particular gifts are portioned out to the members of Christ."

Brothers, 1948), reprinted in 1981 by Christian Classics, Notre Dame, Indiana.

[50] Ibid.

[51] The rest of the quotations in this section are from *ST*, I, Q. 38, art. 2.

ST. BRIGID OF KILDARE: LOVING GIVER OF GIFTS

St. Brigid of Kildare (ca. 452–525) is, with Sts. Patrick and Columba, one of the patrons of Ireland. Born as the illegitimate child of a chieftain and a slave, St. Brigid was best known for her boundless acts of kindness and giving, to the sick and the poor, and even to animals! According to one of many early legends of her compassion, as she cooked up five nice slabs of bacon for her father and four guests, a favorite dog appeared and stared at her with doleful, hungry eyes. Brigid could not help but give the dog a slice of bacon and then a second one for good measure. When a witness told her father, Dubhthach, what had happened, his temper started to flare, but when he asked Brigid if all of the pieces were still there, she asked him to count them, and to his amazement, five juicy pieces remained in the pan!

Because of Brigid's boundless generosity with her (and her father's) possessions, her father eventually decided to give *her* away as a gift to his overlord, Dunglang MacEnda, king of the Province of Leinster. When they arrived, Brigid stayed in the chariot while her father went inside to negotiate. No one carried weapons to a private meeting with the king, so Brigid's father left his prized sword with its jeweled hilt in the chariot with Brigid. While he was inside, a poor leper wandered by, and Brigid had nothing to give him except, as you might surmise, her father's prized sword! When Dubhthach returned, he was so incensed that his sword had been given away that he pulled Brigid back inside before King Dunglang's presence. When the king asked her if she would give away his possessions too, she answered honestly that she would give away all the wealth of Leinster to the poor if it were at her disposal, since she served a higher King. King Dunglang knew well the King whom she served, having been baptized by St. Patrick. He gave Brigid back to her father and gave him an even more valuable sword with an ivory hilt.

As Brigid developed from a young girl to the leader of a growing order of "virgins for Christ," the stories of her generosity never abated, at times alarming even the sisters she had gathered by her open-handed largesse to the poor, due to her complete confidence that the Lord would look after them. Her gifts were not all material either. When Brigid and seven of her sisters shared a meal with the bishop, St. Maccaille, he gave them a discourse on the beatitudes and asked Brigid which of the beatitudes she might choose as the motto for her community. Brigid replied that since there were eight sisters, each should choose one of the beatitudes for her special devotion. The sisters had clearly absorbed Brigid's lessons of humility and generosity, insisting that she choose first. Without hesitation she chose "Blessed are the merciful; for they shall obtain mercy" (Matt. 5:7). Brigid loved her neighbor and was forever immersed in the Corporal and Spiritual Works of Mercy, bringing the gift of Christ's healing to bodies and the gift of forgiveness to souls.

St. Brigid's feast day is February 1.

> *St. Brigid, pray for us. Help us to live lives reflecting the Love and Gift of the Holy Trinity in tender acts of loving care, hospitality, generosity, and mercy.*

CHAPTER 3

ACKNOWLEDGING KNOWLEDGE

Listen to me, my son, and acquire my knowledge, and pay close attention to my words. I will impart instruction by weight, and declare knowledge accurately.

—Sirach 16:24–25

Knowledge is a gift of the Holy Ghost which takes the form of right judgment in things that are to be believed, never confusing them with what ought not to be believed, once the Church has committed itself in deciding which is which.

—Rev. Réginald Garrigou-Lagrange, O.P., *The Theological Virtues*

DO YOU KNOW WHAT KNOWLEDGE IS?

Through the gift of piety we embrace our spiritual sonship or daughterhood. Now it's time to step up another rung of our ladder to listen to the words of our Father and acquire the knowledge He freely offers us. But how will we know whether we have knowledge if we don't know what knowledge is? St. Thomas Aquinas, truly one of the ultimate masters among those who know, has distinguished several kinds of knowledge that God has prepared for us.

We briefly treated of the *intellectual virtue of knowledge* or *science*, whereby, employing our intellectual powers of reason, we, uniquely among all the species on earth, can grasp causes and effects. We can make judgments regarding by what means and relationships things or events come to be and then perhaps exert their own causal powers on other things, causing yet more new outcomes. These judgments of truths about things in the world through discursive, step-by-step rational processes are the stuff of the natural virtue of intellect. The *gift* of knowledge, however, is immeasurably more powerful, more important, and operates in an instant, being guided by the Holy Spirit. As to its swiftness of operation, in exercising the gift of knowledge, we are given the gift of knowing like the angels. Being pure spirit and having no bodies, they do not have to start with information from the senses and move that data, step-by-step to the powers of the rational intellect. Rather, through an illumination from God, angels know what they know intuitively in an instant. The Holy Spirit, of course, knows all things all the time, and when we are blessed by His guidance, the gift of knowledge operates within us in an instant as well. As Thomas has made clear: "God's knowledge is not discursive, or argumentative, but absolute and simple, to which that knowledge is likened to a gift of the Holy Ghost, since it is a participated likeness thereof."[52]

Thomas elaborates that there are two kinds of knowledge that come from the Holy Spirit. The kind of God-given knowledge about matters of belief by which a person knows not only what he should believe but how to convince others of belief and confute those who attack the truths of the Faith is the stuff of the *gratuitous grace* or *charism of knowledge* mentioned by St. Paul in 1 Corinthians 12. God does not give this special gift to everyone, and sometimes to suit His purposes of spreading the Faith, He even gives it to people who are not in a state of grace.

The second kind of knowledge that comes from the Holy Spirit is the gift we are about to unwrap: "a knowledge of what one ought to believe, by discerning things to be believed from things not to be believed: in this way knowledge is a gift and common to all holy persons."[53] The object (or subject matter) of this gift of knowledge is not directly the highest of all causes and the divine things of God, for that is the realm of the gift of wisdom, the crown of all the gifts, which we will address in our final chapter. The gift of knowledge starts us up that ladder toward wisdom by judging of lower causes and effects that are of earthly and human matters, even though it addresses tenets

[52] *ST*, II-II, Q. 9, art. 1.
[53] Ibid.

of the Faith. While the *matters* of faith are themselves divine, the virtue of faith *that dwells within us* is limited, temporal, and exists within the mind of each one of us. The gift of knowledge then helps our minds grasp the ways that creatures imperfectly mirror or reflect their Creator, and it gives us firm judgments about specific articles of faith that Christ's Church on earth has declared to be true and worthy of belief.

When speaking of the intellect, Thomas distinguishes *speculative* operations that strive to contemplate truth in itself and *practical* operations that seek to put truths into action in our lives. The gift of knowledge operates at both of these levels, per Thomas, in an analysis that reflects the Church's great wisdom on the importance of both faith and works. Because its primary subject matter is certitude about the *truths* of the Faith founded upon the *First Truth* of God, the gift of knowledge is principally speculative. But since "the First Truth is also the last end for the sake of which our works are done,"[54] faith extends into works, and as St. Paul wrote in Galatians 5:6, that faith "worketh by charity." Therefore, when we achieve certitude about matters of faith through the gift of the Holy Spirit—let's say about the sanctity of all human life—then this same gift should direct, along with the virtue of charity, the *actions* we take to live out and defend the beliefs that we hold. The knowledge we're given by the Holy Spirit should not be hidden under a basket but should shine forth in visible actions!

KNOWLEDGE OF AND THROUGH THE SACRAMENTS

So how do we get a share of some of this great gift of knowledge? As with all the gifts, of course, we receive it at Baptism, which,

[54] *ST*, II-II, Q. 9, art. 3.

if received as an infant, pretty much coincides with the beginning of our development of natural knowledge about the world around us. If the gift of knowledge operates within us as we grow, we will eventually be able to say of all things in the world "all this is from God" (2 Cor. 5:18) and to attain a deeper grasp of our Faith as our intellects develop. Like other gifts, knowledge is strengthened at the time of Confirmation, when our mental and physical powers have matured as well.

How might the sacrament of Reconciliation help us grow in the gift of knowledge? First of all, through a thorough and heartfelt confession, the mortal sins that shut off the channels of graces, including the gifts, are reopened. Secondly, the gift of knowledge may very well help us to make a good confession if it has prompted us to learn thoroughly the tenets of our Faith, including the thoughts and deeds that are right and wrong in the eyes of God. The gift of knowledge can also enable us to reflect on the world's effects on us — and our effects on others — that might lead to sin. To what extent, for example, are our thoughts, attitudes, and behaviors caused or shaped by the vulgar popular media we might consume? What effects do our words and actions have on those around us? Do they lead others away from God? Through the gift of knowledge we can make a more complete and penetrating examination of conscience.

ARE YOU FASTING FROM THE FEAST THE HOLY SPIRIT HAS PREPARED FOR YOU?

How might our habitual actions hold us back from embracing the gift of knowledge? In a tantalizing theological tidbit, Thomas tells of an insight from Pope St. Gregory the Great: "Knowledge on her own day prepares a feast, because she overcomes the fast of ignorance in the mind."[55] There are times to fast and times to feast, but when it comes to knowledge, the Holy Spirit would have us eat heartily!

Elsewhere in the *Summa Theologica*, Thomas has drawn from the wisdom of "the Philosopher," Aristotle, as well, to show how the vice of *ignorance* opposes the virtue and the gift of knowledge. Aristotle once said that an arrow can miss a target in many ways. If our target is to live in accordance with God's will, we'll also miss the mark if we don't bother to learn God's basic laws of archery. Ignorance in the spiritual sense, then, describes a lack of knowledge of the kinds of things we ought to know. As St. Thomas tells us, "We are all bound in common to know the articles of faith, and the universal principles of right, and each individual is bound to know matters regarding his duty or state."[56] If we don't seek out the knowledge of things we should know, this will indirectly produce sins of omission; if we fail to exercise our minds as we should and to acquire knowledge of the basic truths of the Faith and morals, we will fail to do the good that we could. We will become deficient in how we perform our duties to God, neighbor, and self. If we fail to learn why an act is harmful and sinful, we will be more likely to commit those harmful, sinful acts. Ignorance is decidedly not bliss.

Of course, it is also possible that some of us will seek to banish ignorance and feast upon knowledge, but for a variety of ungodly reasons. And as for some Bonaventurean *bon mots* on improper and proper reasons for seeking knowledge, here — as Thomas borrowed from St. Gregory and Aristotle — Bonaventure shares from the knowledge of St. Bernard of Clairvaux (emphasis added):

[55] Ibid., citing Gregory's *Moralia* 1:32.
[56] *ST*, I-II, Q. 76, art. 2

There are some who wish to know only that they may know; and this is shameful *curiosity*. There are some who wish to know, so that they may be known; and this is shameful *vanity*.... There are some who wish to know, so that they might sell their knowledge for money or honors, and this is *shameful commerce*. There are those who wish to know, so that they might build up others, and this is *charity*. And there are those who wish to know, so that they themselves may be built up. And this is *prudence*.[57]

So we might ask ourselves *why* we want to know. (We hope it is so that our charity and prudence might grow!)

THE SCIENCE OF PRAYING FOR KNOWLEDGE

Sts. Thomas and Bonaventure both preached about how the petitions of the Our Father relate to the gifts of the Holy Spirit. As for the gift of knowledge, both agree that the winner is petition three: "Thy will be done,/ On earth as it is in heaven" (Matt. 6:10).[58] If we are to cooperate with God's will, we need to know just what His will is, through reading Scripture, knowing the deposit of the Catholic Faith as summarized in the *Catechism* and in the sacred liturgies, and heeding the stirrings of the Holy Spirit within our hearts. Notice as well, the reference here to both earth and heaven, since the gift of knowledge pertains to earthly things as they reflect the things of heaven.

Traditional prayers themselves provide a treasury of knowledge of the tenets of the Faith and of how earthly affairs should

[57] St. Bernard's *Sermons on the Song of Songs*, 36, no. 3, cited in St. Bonaventure, *Collations*, p. 103.

[58] *Collations*, p. 48.

be pointed toward heaven as well. To make the effort to learn the words and study the meanings of the great Catholic prayers and creeds is to absorb a great deal of knowledge about the Catholic Faith. In fact, both the *Catechism of the Council of Trent* and our current *Catechism* include detailed expositions of the Profession of Faith and the Lord's Prayer and structure the first and last of their four parts on what we believe and on the nature of Christian prayer. We can do worse with our time than devote it to the memorization of these prayers and the study of the lessons, after invoking the Holy Spirit to guide us. Speaking of which, here is St. Alphonsus Liguori's prayer for the gift of knowledge: "Grant me the gift of knowledge, so that I may know the things of God and, enlightened by Your holy teaching, may walk, without deviation, in the path of eternal salvation."

GETTING TO KNOW THE BLESSINGS AND FRUITS THAT KNOWLEDGE GROWS

We have seen that the gift of knowledge builds upon and perfects the workings of the *intellectual virtue of science* or *knowledge*, which is no surprise, since the virtue relies on the guidance of our reason and the gift relies on the Holy Spirit. St. Thomas tells us that knowledge and understanding are the two gifts that flow from the God-infused, supernatural, *theological virtue of faith*. He echoes the scriptural definition that "faith is the assurance of things hoped for, the conviction of things not seen" (Heb. 11:1). Faith, then, includes a certainty (assurance) and belief (conviction) of the things of God that we are unable to see with our eyes or detect with any of our other senses in our earthly state. What is it that we hope for? Eternal life. What is it that we cannot see? God Himself. And what is the object of certain belief? The ultimate, First Truth, which is God. The gift of knowledge provides us intuitively with a more powerful, steady, and certain belief of the things of God and the articles of faith, even though we may be unable to articulate them in words or defend them completely through rational proofs.

What kind of blessings flow from the insights that the gift of knowledge reveals to us? Interestingly, the first blessing that flows directly from the gift of knowledge is the beatitude of *mourning*. As St. Augustine declared and St. Thomas concurred, when the gift of knowledge has shown us how empty, vain, and worthless earthly goods are in themselves, without their grounding in and reference to God, this insight produces the merit of sorrow when we look back on the errors of our sinful ways and how we have been distracted from God by petty earthly concerns.

A powerful example of this lesson was seen in the life of St. Sylvester Gozzolin (1177–1267) a contemporary of Sts. Thomas and Bonaventure. The saint studied law as a young man, but had a change of heart that led him to the study of theology instead, much to the chagrin of his father, who refused to speak to him for the next ten years. Around the age of fifty, though, St. Sylvester had a deeper conversion, brought about perhaps by a gift of knowledge that completely changed the way that he looked at earthly things. The saint surely knew, just as Abraham did, and as we declare on Ash Wednesday, that we are all but "dust and ashes" (Gen. 18:27), but it was upon seeing the decaying corpse of a woman known for her great beauty in life that Sylvester truly grasped our nothingness without God, realized the vanity of earthly pursuits, and retired to live the life of prayer as a hermit.

What, then, is God's reward for this merit of mourning when we see things as they truly are in themselves? Christ told us: "Blessed are they who mourn, for they shall be comforted" (Matt.

5:4). The reward is comfort, consolation from God that begins even while we sojourn on earth and continues in a perfect and endless state in heaven. As for the fruit of the gift of knowledge, it leads most directly, as you might have surmised, to a more refreshing, enjoyable, and succulent state of *faithfulness*.

THE BLESSED MOTHER AND THE SPIRIT OF KNOWLEDGE

When treating of Mary and the gift of knowledge, Fr. Formby intriguingly and most fittingly begins with God's very first commandment, so to speak, to our first earthly father and mother: "Be fruitful and multiply, and fill the earth and subdue it" (Gen. 1:28). To fill and subdue the earth according to God's will, we need to know how the things of earth relate to God and His plan, and that, of course, as we've seen again and again, is the stuff of the gift of knowledge. Fr. Formby elaborates that the kind of knowledge that man needs to gain dominion over the earth in a godly way requires that he knows God as follows:[59]

- first, as the Divine Source of the power which is needed for government of society
- second, as the Divine Origin of the laws
- third, as the Divine Fountain of the sense of right and wrong
- fourth, as the Supreme Judge, to whose judgment man knows himself to be accountable for his actions, and who is also frequently seen, in the present life, to give such visible effect to His judgments as is proper to maintain His fear among men

---

[59] *Sacrum Septenarium*, 78 (paraphrased here).

Theologians have long called Christ the "new Adam," and Mother Mary the "new Eve," for their roles in our redemption from Adam and Eve's primordial Fall through sin. Blessed Mary possessed the kind of knowledge about God that Fr. Formby stressed as essential, first and foremost because of her knowledge of the story of God and the sacred history of her people through Scripture (at that time, the writings of the Old Testament), made perfect through the gift of the Holy Spirit. Further, she can serve as a motherly example to us to ensure that our own children are educated to know and love the Scriptures and also the subsequent two thousand years of the history of the Christian people, as documented so abundantly in the vast treasury of the Church's written and oral teachings.

HE WHO KNOWS ALL THINGS

St. Thomas posits the puzzling position that Jesus Christ possessed the virtues and the gifts in their fullest perfection — except for the virtues of faith and hope. How could this be? Thomas makes clear that this indicates no lack or deficiency in Christ, but rather quite the contrary. Recall that we read in Hebrews 11:1: "Faith is the assurance of things hoped for, the conviction of things not seen," but it is said of Christ in John 21:17: "Lord, you know everything." Faith and hope pertain to things unseen. Jesus didn't need them, because He already saw all.[60] Yet He did indeed possess the Holy Spirit's gift of knowledge; as we read in Luke 4:1, Jesus was "full of the Holy Spirit." Further, possessing both divine and human natures, Jesus participated in *giving* the

---

[60] *ST*, III, Q. 7, arts. 3, 4.

84

gifts as God and in *receiving* them as man, and possessed both *heavenly knowledge* as God and *earthly knowledge* as man.[61]

Of the many lessons Christ taught us by word and deed that were written down,[62] let's end by pondering one that bears directly on the gift of knowledge by reminding us of the relative value of earthly and heavenly things: "For what shall it profit a man if he gain the whole world and suffer the loss of his soul?" (Mark 8:36, Douay-Rheims).[63]

---

[61] Ibid., art. 5.

[62] Recall that St. John tells us that we know but a small portion right now: "But there are also many other things which Jesus did; were every one of them to be written, I suppose that the world itself could not contain the books that would be written" (John 21:25).

[63] Cf. Matt. 16:26; Luke 9:25.

ST. ALBERT THE GREAT: DOCTOR OF UNIVERSAL KNOWLEDGE

St. Albert of Cologne's (ca. 1200–1280) encyclopedic scientific knowledge was the fruit of a lifetime of study and earned him the title of Magnus (the Great) even while he was alive. The true key to his greatness, though, was the Holy Spirit's gift of knowledge that transformed the great scientist's worldly knowledge into the heavenly knowledge of a great saint.

Albert would become the patron saint of scientists and was the greatest scientist of his day, contributing to every scientific field from A to Z (from anatomy and astronomy to zoology, and virtually every field in between!). It was said that you could repopulate the forests of Bavaria and the river Danube with the animals and the fish he examined in his biological works. To name a few interesting contributions based on his study of nature: he predicted that animals in the extreme north would have white coloring, that there were land masses at the earth's poles, that the visible features on the moon were the moon's own landscape and not reflections of earth's mountains and seas, and that there was a large land mass west of Europe.

Far more important, though, was the fact that through his faith and the Holy Spirit's gift of knowledge, unlike many scientists in our day, Albert knew that all of creation speaks of and reflects the Creator. In his own words: "The first [cause], God — the most true, most sweet, most powerful from eternity, forever and ever and reigning through boundless ages — can be known in another way, that is, though his effects."[64] Albert saw that the world around us is an open book written by and about God. Notice, too, Albert's description of God as "most sweet," revealing the wisdom with which our great saint savored God.[65]

Even more important than Albert's work as a scientist and a philosopher were his works as a theologian. Albert wrote commentaries on several biblical books, most notably on the Gospels, as well as two remarkable books long attributed to him that, even if he did not write them, certainly reflect his concerns and his influence. We already mentioned the paean to the Blessed Mother, the *Mariale*. The other remarkable book is *On Cleaving to God*, and in very Albertian language and themes, it explores how, through ever higher levels of contemplation, the saints surpass the limits and goals of merely intellectual knowledge and seeks no less than loving union with the God they contemplate.

Perhaps of all of St. Albert's great works, the greatest was the work he achieved as a teacher, and the great gift he provided the world was his most promising student, who became perhaps the wisest human teacher the Church has ever called her own.[66]

St. Albert's feast day is November 15.

---

[64] Irven M. Resnick and Kenneth F. Kitchell Jr., trans., *Albert the Great: Questions Concerning Aristotle's* On Animals (Washington, DC: Catholic University of America Press, 2008), 351.

[65] Later we'll examine the sweet connection between savoring and wisdom.

[66] That student's spotlight will come in Profile in Giftedness #7.

St. Albert, pray for us, that through the Holy Spirit's
gift of knowledge, we too may proclaim as you did:
"The whole world is theology for us because
the heavens proclaim the glory of God."[67]

---

[67] From Albert's commentary on Matthew's Gospel as cited in Paul Murray O.P., *The New Wine of Dominican Spirituality: A Drink Called Happiness* (New York: Burns and Oates, 2008), 93.

ANGELIC ANALYSIS #3

THE SPECIAL CHARISMS OF THE HOLY SPIRIT

> To each is given the manifestation of the Spirit for
> the common good. To one is given through the Spirit
> the utterance of wisdom, and to another the utter-
> ance of knowledge according to the same Spirit, to
> another faith by the same Spirit, to another gifts of
> healing by the one Spirit, to another the working of
> miracles, to another prophecy, to another the ability
> to distinguish between spirits, to another various kinds
> of tongues, to another the interpretation of tongues.
> All these are inspired by one and the same Spirit, who
> apportions to each one individually as he wills.
>
> —1 Cor. 12:7–11

As we proceed through our in-depth investigation of each of
the seven gifts of the Holy Spirit, we'll do well to bear in mind
that the Holy Spirit in His divine generosity gives many more
gifts than just those holy seven. The various graces that God so
graciously graces us with are often classified as *sanctifying* graces
(*gratiae gratum faciens*), *personal* graces given to sanctify us so that
we may grow in holiness and in union with God, and *gratuitous*
graces (*gratiae gratis datae*), outward acting ministerial graces
given for the service of others.

Our seven gifts of the Holy Spirit are sanctifying graces given
to all who are open to receiving them. The "special charisms"

enumerated by St. Paul in the opening quotation[68] and explored in this Angelic Analysis are gratuitous graces given only to some for the special purposes of the Holy Spirit, "who apportions to each one individually as he wills" (1 Cor. 12:11). The word *charism* derives from the Greek χάρισμα and is a freely bestowed favor or gratuitous gift. St. Thomas wrote about these charisms in several places in the *Summa Theologica* and elsewhere, and I'll provide just a few highlights so that they may be better understood and distinguished from the seven gifts of the Holy Spirit that lie at the heart of this book.

When preparing to examine the charism of prophecy in depth, St. Thomas provided the quotation from 1 Corinthians 12:7–11 and noted that these various gratuitous gifts or special charisms can be classed into three categories, noting, "Some of them pertain to knowledge, some to speech, and some to operation."[69] Graces pertaining to knowledge all relate in some manner to *prophecy*, and prophecies may relate to matters of *faith*, *wisdom*, *discernment of spirits*, and *knowledge*. Graces pertaining to speech are the abilities to *speak in tongues* and to *interpret tongues*. Graces pertaining to operation are the gifts of *healing* and *miracle working*. Here is a table (culled from *ST*, I-II, Q. 111, art. 4 and Q. 171, art. 2) that lays out St. Thomas's classification scheme based on St. Paul's list:

---

[68] Also discussed in Romans 12 and Ephesians 4 in addition to 1 Corinthians 12.

[69] *ST*, II-II, Q. 171, prologue.

ACKNOWLEDGING KNOWLEDGE

ST. THOMAS ON THE GRATUITOUS GRACES IN 1 CORINTHIANS 12

ST. THOMAS'S CATEGORIES	ST. PAUL'S LIST OF CHARISMS	ST. THOMAS'S DEFINITIONS
Knowledge	Prophecy	A direct gift from God beyond human reasoning powers to foresee future events or to see present or past events "remote from our knowledge"
	Faith	The ability to share with others the certitude about the invisible things, the principles of the Catholic Faith
	Wisdom	The ability to explain to others the knowledge of divine things
	Discernment of spirits	The ability to discern the secrets of others' hearts
	Knowledge	The ability to explain to others how the effects of human, earthly events reflect the causation of God
Speech	Speaking in tongues	The ability to speak in languages that others can understand
	Discernment of tongues	The ability to interpret the sense of what others say

ST. THOMAS'S CATEGORIES	ST. PAUL'S LIST OF CHARISMS	ST. THOMAS'S DEFINITIONS
Operation	Healing	The ability to heal bodily illnesses or infirmities miraculously so as to draw others to the Faith
	Miracle working	The ability to manifest divine power over nature

A look at St. Thomas's classification reveals just what wondrous gifts these are. These charisms burst forth upon the world on Pentecost when the Holy Spirit descended on Mary and the apostles praying in the Upper Room "like the rush of a mighty wind": "And there appeared to them tongues of fire, distributed and resting on each one of them. And they were filled with the Holy Spirit and began to speak in other tongues, as the Spirit gave them utterance" (Acts 2:2–4).

Thomas tells us that the Holy Spirit set the apostles' hearts aflame to fulfill Christ's great commission, "Teach ye all nations."[70] And to see how effectively they took such gratuitous gifts and ran with them, we need only recall the words of St. Augustine: "Whereas even now the Holy Ghost is received, yet no one speaks in the tongues of all nations, because the Church herself already speaks the language of all nations."[71]

[70] *ST*, II-II, Q. 176, art. 1; Matt. 28:19.
[71] *ST*, II-II, Q. 178, art. 1.

PROFILES IN GRACE #3

MOSES, ISAIAH, AND THE CHARISM OF PROPHECY

Ever heard of the prophet Moses? When we think of the biblical prophets, chances are we think of the four major ones (Isaiah, Jeremiah, Ezekiel, and Daniel) and perhaps the twelve minor ones (Hosea, Joel, Amos, Obadiah, Jonah, Micah, Nahum, Habakkuk, Zephaniah, Haggai, Zechariah, and Malachi) whose books appear in the Old Testament. St. Thomas, however, called Moses "simply the greatest of the prophets,"[72] because, like St. Paul, "he saw God's very essence," in seeing the Lord's form clearly (Num. 12:8), because God spoke to Moses "face to face, as a man speaks to his friend" (Exod. 33:11), and because of the miracles that he worked on an entire nation of unbelievers to confirm that his prophecies were of God. As it is written, "And there has not arisen a prophet since in Israel like Moses, whom the LORD knew face to face" (Deut. 34:10).

Thomas noted that God blessed Moses with a special knowledge of the creation of the world, but also that "in some respect one or another of the prophets was greater than Moses."[73] Perhaps one that Thomas had in mind "in some respect" was the prophet Isaiah. It was Isaiah's charism for prophesying that so clearly and beautifully foretold the coming and the life of Christ. Isaiah, of course, has special relevance for us too in our study of

[72] Ibid., Q. 174, art. 4.
[73] Ibid.

the seven gifts of the Holy Spirit, for he prophesied: "There shall come forth a shoot from the stump of Jesse, and a branch shall grow out of his roots. And the Spirit of the LORD shall rest upon him, the spirit of wisdom and understanding, the spirit of counsel and might, the spirit of knowledge and the fear of the LORD. And his delight shall be in the fear of the LORD" (Isa. 11:1–3).

CHAPTER 4

FORTIFYING FORTITUDE

For the thoughts of mortal men are
fearful, and our counsels uncertain.

—Wisdom 9:14, Douay-Rheims

Psalm 67:36 professes: "God is wonder-
ful in his saints; the God of Israel himself
will give power and fortitude to his people."
Therefore, fortitude is a gift of God.

—St. Bonaventure, *Collations on the
Seven Gifts of the Holy Spirit*

IS FORTIFYING FORTITUDE AN EXERCISE IN REDUNDANCY?

The name of the virtue (and gift) of *fortitude*, derives from the Latin word *fortis*, "strength." We see this in many familiar English words. A military stronghold is a called a *fort*, and if we want to strengthen something further, perhaps that fort or even our breakfast cereal, well, we'll *fortify* it with planks and stones, or, in the latter case, with vitamins, in the hope that they will fortify us when we eat them. "Fortifying fortitude" then, means "strengthening strength," but it is clearly not redundant when it comes to the Holy Spirit's gift.

St. Thomas was well aware that some theologians conflated the virtue and the gift, thinking they were but two names for one and the same thing. So, after addressing the *virtue* of fortitude with remarkable thoroughness in a full twelve articles in the *Summa Theologica*,[74] he addresses in two additional articles the *gift* of fortitude and just how it differs from and fortifies the virtue.[75] The natural virtue of fortitude is a "firmness of mind" that allows us to do the good and endure what is evil, especially when our actions involve things that are arduous or difficult.

---

[74] *ST*, II-II, Q. 123. "Of Fortitude" runs eighteen pages in double-column print in the Dominican Fathers' translation.

[75] Ibid., Q. 139, "Of the Gift of Fortitude." (Subsequent citations in this section come from this question's first article.)

Man does possess the capacity to exercise such firmness, both in accomplishing arduous goods and in enduring "grievous evil," and this is the stuff of the virtue of fortitude.

The *gift* of fortitude, however, through the guidance of the Holy Spirit, allows man *not only to struggle to achieve* his ends despite difficulties, but *actually to achieve his final end.* Through virtuous acts of fortitude, perhaps to defend one's loved ones or country, a person might well be thwarted by death, but through the Holy Spirit's gift of fortitude, that person can overcome even death and achieve his ultimate end of everlasting life with God in heaven. Further, the gift can infuse within one's mind "a certain confidence" that will dispel the most powerful fears, as we see in the cases of the holy martyrs, who cherish the gift of fortitude more than even their own bodies.

Our opening quotation makes clear that St. Bonaventure concurs on the special significance of the gift of fortitude over and above the virtue. He starts his lecture on this gift by first describing it "from the perspective of the giver; second from the perspective of the recipient; and finally in terms of the work that comes from it."[76] Then he elaborates, as is characteristic of him, with a wealth of biblical citations and allusions. He expounds on the first point from the perspective of the giver with yet another set of threes: from the perspective of God as Giver, as Redeemer, and as the One who dwells within us.

1. The gift of fortitude is given to us by God, who pro-tects us. Citing Proverbs 18:10, Bonaventure notes: "The name of the Lord is a very strong tower. The just person runs to it and will be exalted."[77] God is the

[76] *Collations*, p. 108.
[77] Ibid.

source of strength that he imputes to all things, and this strength is arranged hierarchically, so that God's strength is also passed down to us through the Church He has established.

2. The gift of fortitude is given to us as well "from God who redeems us through the incarnation of the divine Word. Isaiah 12:2–3 states: "The Lord … is my fortitude and my glory. The Lord has become my salvation. You will draw waters with joy from the fountains of the Savior."[78] He ends by noting that while Christ became weak for our sake, "the weakness of God is stronger than human beings" (see 1 Cor. 1:25).

3. "The third point is that the influence of fortitude comes from God dwelling within us. Thus, Micah 3:8 states: 'I am filled with the strength of the Lord, with judgment, and power.'"[79]

THE GIFT OF SAMSON'S STRENGTH

The biblical Samson's strength was clearly a gift from the Holy Spirit. Indeed, as Samson grew, "the Spirit of the Lord began to stir him" (Judges 13:25), and later we are told that before feats of strength in which he conquered thirty and then a thousand men, "the Spirit of the Lord came mightily upon him" (Judges 14:19; 15:14). With a fascinating exegesis of the holy strong man's story, and how he came to lose the Holy Spirit's graces, St. Bonaventure proceeds to flesh out this third point about the fortitude that arises from God's dwelling within us.

[78] Ibid., p. 109.
[79] Ibid.

To recapitulate the pivotal story in brief: Delilah tries to persuade Samson to reveal the secret of the source of his superhuman strength, which was in his hair that he had never cut. Three times he makes up false stories. He tells her he'll become weak if he is bound with seven cords made of sinews. She has him thus bound when he's asleep and cries out, "The Philistines are upon you, Samson!" He awakens and snaps the cords effortlessly. She asks again, and he clarifies that the cords must be new ones never used before. Again he sleeps, she binds him, calls out, and he breaks free with ease. Delilah is persistent and asks again. Samson tells her the seven locks of his hair must be woven in a web and pinned to the ground, and again the familiar sequence ensues. Delilah is furious and protests that he does not love her because he has not told her the truth. Exasperated, Samson tells her the true story that his strength lies in his hair. Again he sleeps, his hair is cut, and when he wakes to set himself free, not knowing that his hair has been cut, he finds his strength gone. He is then bound and blinded by the Philistines.

Now here is where Bonaventure's intriguing insights come in. He notes that there are four pleasures of the senses by which the gifts of the Holy Spirit are lost: attention, thought, the inclination of the inner affections, and the rejection of the divine laws. The first binding with cords symbolizes the devil's temptation of Samson through the delights of the senses, courtesy of the beautiful Delilah. The second binding with new cords represents how Samson's thoughts have dwelled on sensual delights rather than resisting temptation. The binding of his hair to the ground shows how, through dwelling on those sensual thoughts, his head has become bound to the earth, his mind firmly focused on earthly things. Finally, he was swayed more by love of the beautiful, but treacherous Delilah than by his love of the Lord, and Samson revealed the true secret of the gift of his divine strength, thereby rejecting the divine law. The result was, to his surprise, loss of the Holy Spirit's special gift of his superhuman strength. Notice too there are *seven* cords to bind him, and indeed, in the words of Scripture, Samson's strength from the Lord was in "the *seven* locks of his head" (Judges 16:19, emphasis added), signifying, as Bonaventure notes, "the seven-fold grace of the Holy Spirit."[80]

Readers of Scripture will likely recall that, while he was bound and blind, Samson's hair grew back, perhaps as he grew to see again with the eyes of faith and his heart grew strong again in his love of the Lord. When the Philistines gathered to sacrifice to their god Dagon for handing over Samson to them, Samson called on the Lord once again and asked Him to strengthen him one last time. Blessed again with his old strength, he knocked over the house's pillars, destroying the enemies of God, even though he knew he too would die when the house collapsed. What a fascinating lesson on the gifts of the Holy Spirit in action, especially the gift of fortitude that can lead a strong man even to forfeit his life in the service of God!

THE SACRAMENT OF FORTITUDE

Although none of the seven sacraments is named fortitude, one has a particularly powerful link to the gift of fortitude: Confirmation. St. Thomas wrote that "Confirmation is to Baptism as growth is to birth,"[81] and as we grow bigger, we grow stronger. The *Catechism* tells us "by the sacrament of Confirmation,

---

[80] Ibid., p. 111.
[81] *ST*, III, Q. 72, art. 6.

[the baptized] are more perfectly bound to the Church and are enriched with a special strength of the Holy Spirit" (no. 1285). Whereas the sacrament strengthens us in all of the gifts of the Holy Spirit, it provides us with a special strength of the Holy Spirit to spread and defend the Faith (no. 1303).

The minister of this sacrament is the bishop, who lays hands on the recipient, anoints him with chrism, and pronounces the words of the rite of Confirmation, invoking the spiritual seal of the Holy Spirit. Why does the bishop administer Confirmation, while priests administer Baptism? "Though he who is baptized is made a member of the Church, nevertheless he is not yet enrolled as a Christian soldier. And therefore he is brought to the bishop, as to the commander of the army."[82] Just look at today's headlines;[83] you cannot ignore the fact that the Church is under attack by a variety of secular forces, and Christians in parts of the world are being attacked, driven from their lands, and even martyred in numbers unseen for hundreds of years. Indeed, we all need to "put on the whole armor of God" (Eph. 6:11), and "fight the good fight of the faith" (1 Tim. 6:12) in ways we may not have imagined even a few years ago. *Lord, give us the strength of the gift of fortitude!*

There is another sacrament that can fortify us too, and we may receive it often. Every time we receive the Eucharist, we receive that kind of fortitude that comes, as St. Bonaventure said, "from God dwelling within us."

---

[82] Ibid., art. 10.

[83] Today (June 20, 2016) I read a headline about a Spanish cardinal threatened with a legal suit for a "hate crime," for proclaiming clear Catholic sexual morality in defense of the traditional family.

FORTIFYING FORTITUDE

ARE YOU CHOOSING WEAKNESS OVER STRENGTH?

Fortitude is the guardian of the virtues, and the gift of fortitude ratchets up the defenses to make them impenetrable when it is deployed. In what ways might we be sabotaging our own defenses?

Aristotle, and St. Thomas following him, spoke of the moral virtues as "golden means," dispositions to act in just the right manner, situated at just the right distance between the vices of deficiency on one side and the vices of excesses on the other.

Fearfulness or moral weakness opposes fortitude as a deficiency, while a foolhardy *fearlessness* and reckless *daring* oppose fortitude as vices of excess. There are some souls so overblown with temerity that they distort the strength of fortitude by taking unnecessary risks, "jumping in where angels fear to tread," and ignoring the wisdom of Sirach (13:2): "Do not lift a weight beyond your strength." Far more common, though, is that vice of deficiency, the disposition toward timidity and fearfulness that may come to guide our actions (or lack thereof) when situations arise in which we should defend the Faith and stand up and speak out for what we know is right.

Although this is not the place for a detailed examination of what St. Thomas called the "integral parts" of the *virtue* of fortitude,[84] they bear a brief mention before we zoom in on the *gift*. In terms of the kinds of positive attitudes and actions that are required for the virtue of fortitude to flourish, we find the virtues of *magnanimity*, literally "greatness of soul,"[85] that guides our thoughts and actions to great and not petty things, to things that truly matter and are truly honorable, even though they may

---

[84] Interested readers may note that I have addressed them extensively in chapter 4 of *Unearthing Your Ten Talents*.

[85] From the Latin *magnus* (great) and *anima* (soul).

be difficult to obtain. The magnanimous person seeks lofty goals and is not disturbed if others do not understand or approve, as long as he knows that what he's seeking is morally right and consistent with the Faith.

The other positive virtue aligned with fortitude is that of *magnificence*, the habitual tendency to try to make or build great things,[86] even if this requires a great outlay of money, for example, in the construction of a church, a school, a hospital, a Catholic radio or TV station or network, or any grand, worthwhile project. Through fortitude we overcome undue fears of threats to our bodies and souls; through magnificence we overcome undue threats to our wallets! Recalling that the gift of fortitude perfects the natural virtue of fortitude, we might ask ourselves if we have given the gift a good base to build upon.

Rather than growing in magnanimity, have we allowed ourselves to become overly influenced by our modern culture and mired in the *pusillanimity*, "smallness of soul," that focuses too much on the petty things of the world? Or have we overshot the mark, falling prey to the kind of *presumption*, *ambition*, or *vainglory* through which we treat as great not the things of God but our own thoughts, desires, and thirst for fame or power?

Rather than displaying magnificence and contributing generously to the needs of the Church, have we fallen prey to the vice of stinginess or meanness, contributing little to noble projects, while perhaps at the same time, displaying the vice of *consumption*, or waste, spending money extravagantly on things that don't really matter, just to satisfy our whims or to build our reputations?

Even more central to fortitude than these allied positive virtues that guide us toward the right actions are two virtues that

---

[86] From the Latin *magnus* (great) and *facere* (to do or make).

perfect fortitude's capacity to endure.[87] The first allied virtue is the *patience* whereby we endure the sufferings produced by others or by events outside our control without giving in to sorrow and defeat and without lashing out inappropriately. The second allied virtue is the *perseverance* whereby we endure in virtuous thoughts and behaviors even when the going gets tough and stays tough, and when our attempts to achieve virtuous goals are met by obstacles and delays. In the grandest sense, perseverance comes into play as we try to persevere in the practice of our Faith throughout our lifetime, for as St. Matthew tells us, "He who endures to the end will be saved" (Matt. 24:13). So we might ask ourselves if we have built up or undermined our capacities to endure in fortitude.

Rather than growing in patience in dealing with a difficult situation or a difficult person, have we demonstrated instead *impatience* by lashing out at the person or perhaps by fleeing the situation, such as refusing to care for a loved one because of his abrasive words or actions toward us? Have we demonstrated *resignation* by staying the course, but in a spirit of sadness or defeat? Have we overshot the golden mean of patience by an undue *subservience*, perhaps by actively seeking out and staying in abusive relationships, displaying what is sometimes called "doormat" behavior in modern parlance, allowing ourselves to be stepped on by others without a reasonable word of complaint? Have we displayed what we might call *"pseudo-martyrdom"* by willfully seeking out such relationships with others that produce obstacles to our own good, and then complaining of the pains we must endure to all who will hear us?

---

[87] In St. Thomas's own words, "Now the principal act of fortitude is to endure." *ST*, II-II, Q. 123, art. 8.

Clearly there are many questions we might ask ourselves as to how we might undermine the walls to our souls that are guarded by the virtue of fortitude, but what about the gift? Well, the gift builds upon the virtue, so all the same questions are still worth the asking. As for other obstacles contrary to the gift, I direct readers back to St. Bonaventure's analysis of Samson. Samson's strength and courage were unmatched, but when he diverted his attention to worldly pleasures and dwelled on them in thought until they replaced God at the center of his heart, he unwittingly, in a sense, chose to forgo the Holy Spirit's mighty gifts. Of course, even in his life we see the true merciful nature of the Holy Spirit as Love and Gift. For when Samson repented, those "seven locks" began to grow once again and God answered his prayer for new strength.

THE POWER OF PRAYER FOR POWER

The first prayer that comes to my mind when I think of the gift of fortitude is the simple oft-heard "Lord, give me strength!" In fact, there is nothing at all wrong with short, sweet prayers like that to call upon God at times when we face life's difficulties and could use some instantaneous spiritual fortification.

Sts. Thomas and Bonaventure concur that the petition in the Lord's Prayer "Give us this day our daily bread" pertains to the gift of fortitude. Bonaventure explains that this is because bread "strengthens the human heart,"[88] echoing Psalm 104:15, and Thomas chimes in that "this gift of fortitude prevents man's heart from fainting through fear of lacking necessities, and makes him trust without wavering that God will provide

---

[88] *Collations*, p. 49.

him with whatever he needs. For this reason the Holy Spirit, the giver of this fortitude, teaches us to pray to God to *give us this day our daily bread.*"[89] Theologians have long noted deeper meanings involving the bread in this petition, and Thomas explains that it also refers to the *sacramental bread* that is the Eucharist and to "the Word of God: 'Not by bread alone doth man live but by every word that proceedeth from the mouth of God.' "[90] Those words were spoken to Satan by Him who is "the living bread which came down from heaven" (John 6:51). When the devil tries our fortitude, we might both echo Christ's words and heed His advice with hearty daily servings of the bread of Scripture!

Let's conclude here with St. Alphonsus Liguori's petition: "Grant me the spirit of fortitude that I may bear my cross with Thee, and that I may overcome with courage all the obstacles that oppose my salvation."

THE BLESSINGS AND GIFTS FORTITUDE FOSTERS

St. Thomas defends St. Augustine's precedent in his writings on the Sermon on the Mount in matching the gifts to the Beatitudes in the order in which they are listed in Scripture and finding fitting correspondences between them. Augustine, therefore, matched the fourth beatitude of *hungering and thirsting after justice* to the fourth gift of fortitude. Thomas acknowledges that while the gift of piety is related to the virtue of justice,

---

[89] St. Thomas Aquinas, *The Aquinas Catechism: A Simple Explanation of the Catholic Faith by the Church's Greatest Theologian* (Manchester, NH: Sophia Institute Press, 2000), 137.
[90] Ibid., 141, citing Matt. 4:4.

fortitude is about difficult things, and it is very difficult not only to do virtuous deeds in accord with justice, "but furthermore to do them with an unsatiable desire, which may be signified by hunger and thirst for justice." (I don't know about you, but when I read of such an unquenchable desire for justice despite the most enormous of difficulties, my thoughts turn to the gift of fortitude so mightily displayed in the works of St. Teresa of Calcutta.)

As for the fruits that fortitude fosters, St. Thomas suggests *patience*, which endures evils, and *longanimity* (perseverance), which holds up over long delays to accomplish worthwhile goods.

THE FORTITUDE OF THE BLESSED MOTHER

What could be more difficult for a loving mother to bear than the torture and execution of her child, and how could she bear this without the Holy Spirit's gift of fortitude? Fr. Formby recalls the example of Hagar, Abraham's maid who bore him the child Ishmael. Hagar and Ishmael were sent away, and their water ran out as they wandered in the wilderness. Presuming her son would die, Hagar laid him under a bush and went away about the distance of a bowshot, saying, "Let me not look upon the death of the child" (Gen. 21:16), but God intervened to save them. The Blessed Mother, on the contrary, was blessed with the fortitude to stand close by the Cross and witness with her eyes the suffering and death of her innocent Son because she knew it was His will and God's plan. Perhaps her example of holy fortitude could help give us the strength to stand by and not flee from the sufferings of our loved ones as they approach the ends of their lives on earth.

FORTIFYING FORTITUDE

THE FORTITUDE OF THE CROSS

Of course, it was the ultimate act of fortitude to experience those physical sufferings that Mary observed, knowing as well that His Mother's love and fortitude allowed her to be there for Him to the gruesome end of His earthly mission, despite all the sorrow she suffered. The human natural virtue of fortitude, as we have seen, has its limits. Christ prayed, "My Father, if it be possible, let this cup pass from me; nevertheless, not as I will, but as thou wilt" (Matt. 26:39), and yet through the Holy Spirit's gift of unfailing fortitude, Christ drank the suffering of that cup dry, as His Father had willed, so that through His Passion, death, and Resurrection we would have the chance to persevere to the end and share in eternal bliss with the Holy Trinity and to say, like St. Paul, "I can do all things in him who strengthens me" (Phil. 4:13).

ST. IGNATIUS OF ANTIOCH: GOD'S WHEAT

The world's eyes are focused today on atrocities in Syria. Brutality abounded there nineteen hundred years ago as well, but the land was also blessed with an enduring model of saintliness in the person of Antioch's second bishop, Ignatius (ca. 35–ca.108), who would become among the Church's greatest of early martyrs.

During the reign of the powerful and far-reaching Roman emperor Trajan, Bishop Ignatius of Antioch was arrested and sentenced to death for refusing to renounce his faith in Christ. On the long journey to Rome, accompanied by ten fierce "leopards" (Roman soldiers), Ignatius penned seven letters explaining and defending the truths of the Faith — from its universality (with the first use of the term *catholic* for the Church), to Christ's presence in the Eucharist, to the Church's hierarchy and the authority of bishops — and providing one of the most powerful, enduring models of the undefeatable strength of the Holy Spirit's gift of fortitude.

Ignatius looked his death sentence squarely in the face and did not balk in the slightest, knowing he would be fed to wild animals in Rome. Indeed, he wrote to the Romans that he went willingly, and he dissuaded them from trying to prevent his martyrdom. He wrote them: "Permit me to be food for the beasts; through them I will reach God. I am the wheat of God and I compete through the beasts to be found the pure bread of Christ."[91] Indeed, he notes

---

[91] Ignatius, Letter to the Romans 4:2 as cited in Kenneth Howell, *Ignatius of Antioch: A New Translation and Theological Commentary* (Zanesville, OH: CHResources, 2008), 96.

that if the animals are too shy to touch him, he will provoke them, their bodies becoming his tomb.

Clearly, St. Ignatius's remarkable fortitude far exceeded the bounds of natural virtue and bespoke of a mighty stirring of the Holy Spirit. Ignatius was spurred by the spirit of the gift of fortitude to interpret his painful journey and martyrdom as a means to complete union with Christ. Dr. Howell elaborates on the relationship between the Eucharist and martyrdom for St. Ignatius, noting that, in receiving sacramental Communion, a person becomes more a disciple of Christ and grows in desire to be with Christ. Martyrdom provides the means for the union in reality. "The martyr's heart then finds its fulfillment in full union with Jesus Christ in which he becomes the same reality he receives in the Eucharist and so can be called the bread of God."[92]

St. Ignatius became the food of lions and the bread of God in the Roman Coliseum, in or shortly after the year 108.

St. Ignatius's feast day is October 17.

St. Ignatius of Antioch, pray for us, that embracing the Holy Spirit's gift of fortitude, and nourished by the body, blood, soul, and divinity of Christ, we too may persevere in the Faith with hope and with joy, regardless of the persecutions we may be called to endure.

---

[92] Ibid., footnote.

ANGELIC ANALYSIS #4

NATURAL AND SUPERNATURAL VIRTUES

> Virtue denotes a certain perfection of a power. Now a
> thing's perfection is considered chiefly in regard to its
> end. But the end of power is act. Wherefore power is said
> to be perfect, according as it is determinate to its act....
> But the rational powers, which are proper to man, are
> not determinate to one particular action, but are inclined
> indifferently to many; and they are determinate to acts by
> means of habits.... Therefore human virtues are habits.
>
> —St. Thomas Aquinas, *Summa Theologica*, I-II, Q. 55, art. 1

There's a lot to unwrap in our opening quotation, and that is the
end of this chapter, as I'll hope to make clear from its very start!
Recall that in the opening quotation of our introduction Thomas
mentioned that virtues perfect man according to natural human
reason, and the gifts of the Holy Spirit provide even "higher
perfections" that come from God and that make our actions
amenable to "divine inspiration." And recall that Thomas noted
that whereas virtues counter vice and sin, the gifts assist even
virtues in making up for any "defects."[93]

The word *virtue* derives from the Latin *vir*, "man," and in
Aristotle's Greek, the word *arête* was used, indicating "excellence." Virtues, then, allow us to become excellent—more fully

---

[93] "The gifts are bestowed to assist the virtues and to remedy certain defects ... so that, seemingly, they accomplish what the
virtues cannot." *ST*, I-II, Q. 68, art. 8.

and perfectly human — by disposing us to perform good acts, to perfect ourselves, and to give the best of ourselves. When we possess the virtues, it becomes easier and more natural and enjoyable for us to do the right things. We're able to maximize our human powers. Virtues make us and our actions good.

Those fundamental human powers include the abilities to *desire* and to *will*, to discern what we seek to enjoy or to avoid, and to choose freely whether we will pursue those desires. Since our natures are fallen, our desires by themselves are no sure guide to excellence and happiness. If we are to exercise virtue, our desires and choices must be guided by *reason* (and for Christians, as we'll see, by our *faith* as well). This perfection of our thinking, desiring, and choosing is the stuff of the virtues, those peaks of excellence that crown our human natures and point us toward heaven.

THE VIRTUES OF NATURE

Aristotle noted long ago that "goodness has two forms, moral virtue and intellectual excellence, for we praise not only the just but also the intelligent and the wise."[94] He (and St. Thomas) addressed three so-called intellectual virtues that perfect our human reasoning abilities: *science* or *knowledge* (recall that *science* comes from the Latin *scire*, "to know"), *understanding*, and *wisdom*. In a nutshell, the virtue of science relates to the grasp of cause-and-effect relationships, understanding pertains to the comprehension of fundamental and overarching principles, and wisdom pertains to the highest of intellectual activities, "containing beneath itself understanding and science, by judging both

[94] *Eudemian Ethics*, II, 1, 19.

the conclusions of science and of the principles on which they are based," per St. Thomas.[95]

These intellectual virtues help us to attain the truth. They were valued by the writers of the Old Testament, where we see them all together, for example, in Proverbs 24:3–5: "By wisdom a house is built, and by understanding it is established; by knowledge the rooms are filled with all precious and pleasant riches. A wise man is mightier than a strong man, and a man of knowledge than he who has strength."

The intellectual virtues perfect the powers of our "speculative intellect" so that we may *know what is true,* and the *moral* virtues act to perfect our wills and appetites, or passions, so that we may *do what is good.* Four of these moral virtues, called the *cardinal* virtues, from the Latin *cardine,* "hinge," have long been considered of fundamental importance for all other moral virtues "hinge," or depend, on them.

- *Prudence* (practical wisdom) harnesses our reason, will, and appetites to employ virtuous means to achieve virtuous goals.
- *Fortitude* reins in, with reason, our irascible appetite so that we may overcome obstacles to the goods we seek.
- *Temperance* reins in, with reason, our concupiscible appetite through which we seek out what we see as good.
- *Justice* reins in, with reason, our will so that we give to each person his rightful due.

St. Thomas tells us, "Human virtues are habits." He used the word *habitus,* which we translate merely as "habit" at the risk of missing out on the full richness of Thomas's meaning, for the

---

[95] *ST,* I-II, Q. 57, art. 2.

habits of virtue are far more than reflexive, unthinking ways of acting that we happened to have acquired over time.

Rather, habits that are natural virtues are dispositions or inclinations to seek out the truth and to do the good that we build within ourselves through repeated practice. In essence, good habits are to virtues as bad habits are to vices, vices being tendencies we build within ourselves to follow our passions and whims, even when our reason bids us to hold back. Sins, then, are literally vicious acts (acts of vice), whereas good deeds are virtuous acts (acts in accord with or sprouting forth from virtue).

So then, how might we, by our own efforts, strive to perfect our soul's powers with virtue, rather than have our soul's powers perverted by vice?[96] Well, as Aristotle once famously wrote, "We become builders by building and harpists by playing the harp." So too can we build natural virtues within our souls by simply *doing* virtuous acts regularly and repeatedly. But you might ask, "How, then, can I *do* virtuous acts to *become* virtuous if I am not already virtuous in the first place?" Good question—sort of!

This might seem like a chicken-and-egg situation. In order to perform virtuous actions, wouldn't we already have to be virtuous? Partially, but not entirely. How does a weightlifter acquire the strength to lift enormous weights? He starts by lifting much lighter weights and then uses progressively heavier weights over time as he grows stronger and stronger. He starts with the muscles that nature provided him; then he perfects them through his habitual actions. Nature has provided us with all the necessary initial dispositions to virtue. As we've already seen, we all have appetites, passions, reason, and will. Now,

---

[96] The latter, alas, seems the goal of so much advertising, popular entertainment, and political propaganda in our day.

what are we going to *do* with them? To turn these potentialities, these capacities that dispose us toward the good, into full-blown natural virtues, we must perform virtuous acts again and again. As St. Thomas put it, "A disposition becomes a habit, just as a boy becomes a man."[97]

Note too, that virtues, when developed, make it easier for us to make the right choices in the future, since such choices have become, well, good habits.

THE NATURAL VIRTUES

CATEGORY	POWER	VIRTUE
Intellectual virtues	Speculative intellect	Understanding
		Science
		Wisdom
	Practical intellect	Art (A virtue of the practical intellect, art was not classified as one of the fundamental intellectual or moral virtues described by St. Thomas.)

[97] *ST*, I-II, Q. 49, art. 2.

CATEGORY	POWER	VIRTUE
Moral virtues		Prudence (Although part of the practical intellect, prudence guides the will and the lower appetites and is therefore, in a sense, both an intellectual and a moral virtue, since it seeks true means to achieve goods.)
	Will (or intellectual appetite)	Justice
	Concupiscible appetite	Temperance
	Irascible appetite	Fortitude

THE VIRTUES OF A SUPERNATURE

Ancient pagan philosophers thought that the natural virtues were the be-all and end-all of human perfections. They either lived too far back in time to know or were not aware that one day in Bethlehem, the source and fount of all virtue, indeed, of all that is, took on human flesh to raise us to heights we had not conceived, from our earthly natures all the way to heaven. God's Word Incarnate, Jesus Christ, came to earth, lived and died for our sins, and with the Father and Holy Spirit has graced us with "super virtues," so to speak, that exceed our human natures because they are infused in our souls by God Himself when we accept Him. These are called the *supernatural*, or *theological*, virtues, and St. Paul enumerated them as faith, hope, and love.

Once these virtues have captured our minds and our hearts, they guide and perfect both the moral and the intellectual virtues and direct all our powers to the things of God. St. Paul writes of these virtues most poignantly in 1 Corinthians 13, where he explains that one of them towers over the other two and will last even in heaven. In heaven we won't need faith in God, because we will see Him and be with Him. Nor will we need hope that we will achieve heaven and that God will supply us with the assistance to get there, because we will already be there.

"Love never ends," though, explains St. Paul, and "the greatest of these is love" (1 Cor. 13:8, 13). This love, or charity, will endure eternally as we live and love in the presence of God, the angels, and the Communion of Saints, and it begins here on earth when we accept God and His love in our hearts. St. Paul has told us what this love is like (patient, kind, rejoicing in the right, bearing all things, believing all things, hoping for all things, enduring all things) and what it is not like (jealous, boastful, arrogant, rude, insisting on its own way, irritable, or rejoicing at wrong) (see 1 Cor. 13:4–7).

These supernatural, theological virtues serve to unite us to God, to make us His sons and daughters, and to allow us to share

His love with others. And yet, as awesome and "super" as these supernatural virtues that God infuses into our souls are, He gives us still more with the gifts of the Holy Spirit.

PROFILE IN GRACE # 4

ARISTOTLE AND CICERO

There is absolutely no difficulty in finding saints to illustrate the virtues. After all, any person declared Venerable on the path toward canonization must have displayed the theological and cardinal virtues in his life to a "heroic degree." I will highlight Aristotle and Cicero for our purposes, though, even though both were pagan philosophers who died before the birth of Christ.

Greatly gifted by God in natural intelligence and possessed by the desire to learn, Aristotle (384–322 BC) exercised the natural intellectual virtues to previously unheard of heights as the Father of Logic, who would be described by the likes of Sts. Albert, Thomas, and Bonaventure as simply "the Philosopher." He was of particular importance to Christian theologians because of the way his reason led him to the steadfast conclusion that God truly must exist, because of his depth of understanding of human cognition and emotion, and for the way his reason penetrated many truths about the nature of natural virtues, thus paving the way for a deeper Christian understanding of the theological virtues and gifts that would perfect them.

Marcus Tullius Cicero (106–43 BC), the great Roman states-man, orator, and philosopher, would also profoundly influence great Catholic thinkers who would go on to explain the gifts. We have addressed St. Jerome's dream that he was whipped by an angel for following Cicero more closely than he followed Christ. St. Augustine reported that he was drawn to the study of philosophy by Cicero, and Sts. Albert the Great and Thomas Aquinas borrowed freely and with full acknowledgment from the way he described the cardinal virtues and their parts. Cicero displayed the heights of personal fortitude on December 7, 43 BC, when he offered his head to the soldier whom Marc Antony had sent to retrieve it (along with his hands) for daring to think and to write about freedom from tyranny.

May we learn from the examples of Aristotle and Cicero how to make the most of the mental and moral capacities God has given us, and may we keep in mind that as Christians we have greater gifts yet that we may employ in this regard than either of them every fully realized.

CHAPTER 5

COUNTING ON COUNSEL

Reason is the beginning of every work, and
counsel precedes every undertaking.

—Sirach 37:16

The gift of counsel is about what has to be
done for the sake of the end.

—St. Thomas Aquinas, *Summa Theologica*, II-II, Q. 52, art. 2

COUNSEL'S PLACE IN THE HOLY GIFT SET

The gifts of the Holy Spirit are like a "gift set," each gift so perfectly complementing the others. The gifts of fear, piety, and fortitude all direct our affective appetites to the things we desire or dread, the things we will to achieve or to avoid.[98] The gift of knowledge was the first gift we examined that serves to perfect the intellect in its tasks of knowing the true nature of created things and of correctly judging matters of the Faith. Now the Holy Spirit has provided yet another gift, our fifth of the seven "spirits": the spirit or gift of counsel, which guides and directs these other gifts. We know that we are to fear the Lord, to revere Him as our Father and love our neighbors as brothers and sisters, and to trust in Him to give us the knowledge to know the true nature and value of things and the courage to defend what is right, regardless of its cost to us. But we still require special guidance from above to grasp the right means to achieve those holy goals, to feel certain that we have ascertained those right means, and to put them into action at the right time and in the right way. This is the stuff of the great gift of counsel.

---

[98] Note in the second table in the appendices that the gift of fear directs our concupiscible appetite to the things we desire, the gift of fortitude directs our irascible appetite in avoiding or combating dangers, and the gift of piety directs our wills in matters pertaining to how we relate to others.

St. Thomas begins his discussion of the gift of counsel by distinguishing it from the virtue of prudence and from its allied virtue of counsel. Prudence, as we saw in the Angelic Analysis essay #4, is that cardinal virtue of practical wisdom that seeks out and implements rational means to rational ends, and it operates through the assistance of a series of other virtues and capacities.[99] Further, natural prudence may receive assistance through additional virtues, which St. Thomas called "potential parts," that guide it in particular matters. The most relevant one for our purposes is that of *eubolia* (good counsel), which Thomas defines as a natural "disposition to take good counsel"[100] or advice from others about how to achieve virtuous goals. So what more does a person need to make and act on prudent decisions? Well, to ensure that our plans are prudent and that the counsel we may have received is truly good, and to know these facts with a sense of certainty, we need that gift of counsel that transcends our own and others' human reason and that comes from the stirrings of the Holy Spirit.

Human reason is unable to know perfectly all the singular circumstances or contingencies surrounding any potential course of action, but the Holy Spirit knows all and can give us the counsel that perfects our imperfect attempts at applying universal moral principles to specific situations through the use of practical reasoning. The Holy Spirit has the power in even the most difficult of situations to find virtuous means to virtuous ends, either by guiding our minds directly, or by guiding us to

---

[99] St. Thomas describes eight "integral parts" required to exercise the virtue of prudence fully: memory, understanding, docility, shrewdness, reason, foresight, circumspection, and caution. *ST* II-II, Q. 49. I've also addressed each of these in detail in *Unearthing Your Ten Talents*.

[100] *ST*, II-II, Q. 51, art. 1.

seek counsel from appropriate advisers. Counsel, then, is the gift that gets things done!

John of St. Thomas also distinguishes the gift of counsel from "practical faith," the kind that is enlivened by the virtue of charity, noting that it is not sufficient in and of itself to accomplish what is done by the virtue of counsel:

Faith is only practical in an eminent way as a higher and universal rule, not as a proximate rule applicable to works of the moment. Faith does not supply judgment of the means to be chosen. For such a judgment requires a more determined and particular virtue, a virtue which does not merely believe what ought to be known and done. This virtue must also discern and judge the means and manner of acting, the amount of intention and effort, the time, the measure, and such like. Faith does not treat of all these particulars.[101]

The gift of counsel "is like the prudence of the Spirit,"[102] says John of St. Thomas, noting that the intellectual gifts of knowledge, understanding, and wisdom in turn guide the gift of counsel, as they provide the *practical principles* "in an abstract and scientific way," that counsel then takes and runs with, applying those principles to concrete specific actions and real-life situations.

SACRAMENTS OF COUNSEL

Of course, as the case is for all of the gifts, we receive the gift of counsel at Baptism, and it is strengthened in us at Confirmation.

[101] *The Gifts of the Holy Ghost*, p. 161.
[102] Ibid., 162.

When we go to Confession, in addition to the remission of our sins, we may well receive counsel from the priest in the person of Christ, in the form of either spiritual advice or appropriate acts of penance.

And speaking of the priest, St. Thomas has noted that "the sacraments of the New Law cause what they signify. Now [Orders] by their sevenfold number signify the seven gifts of the Holy Ghost.... Therefore the gifts of the Holy Ghost which are not apart from sanctifying grace, are given in Orders." When God gives the priest the power to administer the "sevenfold" sacraments, He renews in him the gifts of the Holy Spirit too, including that of counsel.

And what about the people who are blessed to receive the sacrament of Matrimony? I would opine that they have been open to the Holy Spirit's gift of counsel in guiding them to a spouse who can, in turn, provide them with good human counsel! On a broader and very timely note as well, we should recall St. Thomas's words on the very nature of marriage and on its early origin: "Matrimony was instituted for the begetting of children. But the begetting of children was necessary to man before sin. Therefore it behooved Matrimony to be instituted before sin."[103] How interesting that this great gift of God, marriage between one man and one woman, is literally older than sin!

THE COUNSELS OF PERFECTION (AND BAD COUNSELORS WHO OPPOSED THE ANGELIC AND SERAPHIC DOCTORS)

The gift of counsel is clearly essential to all of us, regardless of our state of life. But for a specific state of life, that of the avowed

---

[103] *ST*, Supplement, Q. 42, art. 2.

members of religious orders, spiritual perfection is sought through what are called the "evangelical counsels" or "counsels of perfection." Although Christ gave precepts and commandments that all Christians must heed, these three higher perfections of *chastity*, *poverty*, and *obedience* derive from the counsels that Christ gave to those who asked Him the means of spiritual perfection: when He told the rich man, "If you would be perfect, go, sell what you possess and give it to the poor"; when He spoke of "eunuchs for the sake of the kingdom of heaven"; and when He advised that we seek not worldly honor and power because "many that are first will be last, and the last first" (Matt. 19:21, 12, 30).

It was St. Francis of Assisi (1182–1226) who first initiated these three counsels of poverty, chastity, and obedience as part of the religious vows for his Order of Friars Minor, and it is interesting to note that in his sermons on the gifts, Francis's own biographer and the eighth minister general of his Franciscan Order, our own guide St. Bonaventure, brings up these vows to uphold the counsels as practiced by both the Franciscans and the Dominicans.

In fact, both young orders had come under attack for their novel ways and for not embracing the older monastic practice of "stability," staying in one place like monks; instead they traveled around to preach and spread the Gospel, embracing the counsels of poverty, chastity, and obedience. Some called them "counterfeit" orders and tried to drive them from settings such as the University of Paris, where both Bonaventure and Thomas taught. In any event, Bonaventure declared that those who attacked the Franciscans and the Dominicans were examples of the kinds of bad counselors whom the gift of counsel gives us guidance to avoid! "The Pharisees and Lawyers were counselors of this type. Of them it is said in Luke 7:30: 'The Pharisees and lawyers rejected the counsel of God.' "[104] Drawing broader lessons from this example, Bonaventure also cites the counsel of Sirach 6:6: "Live in peace with many, but let one in a thousand be your counselor."[105]

ARE YOU LISTENING TO THE STILL, SMALL VOICE OF COUNSEL?

We will not be receptive to the Holy Spirit's gift of counsel if we are too busy listening to the bad counselors of the world or to our own voices, for that matter. While the world erupted around him in violent tumult, the prophet Elijah retired to a cave in Mount Horeb, the "mount of God." Elijah witnessed powerful winds that rent mountains, an earthquake, and then a great fire, "but the Lord was not in [them]." But after the fire came "a still, small voice," and Elijah then went out to converse with the Lord, who instructed him where to go and what to do next. Perhaps we can learn from Elijah's example always to keep our ears open to that "still, small voice" that is still there to provide us with direction in our lives. To do so, perhaps we would be wise to turn off at times the barrage of competing voices that bombard us today through electronic devices.

In a lecture on the gift of counsel in the 1990s, Cardinal Martini revealed that he had provided counsel for more than a thousand youths as they discerned their vocations in life. He described the all-too-common problem of procrastination, through which many young people fritter away their time, avoiding important decisions: "When one puts off decisions because one does not know what to do and prefers not to think about it, when one goes

[104] *Collations*, p. 155. Cf. Luke 7:30.
[105] *Collations*, p. 152.

ahead under the illusion that someone will tell you what to do, all this signifies that the gift of counsel is lacking."[106]

Perhaps not surprisingly, he advised these youths to undertake ascetical exercises of prayer and reflection, but, also quite intriguingly, he asked them to follow two rules: "to renounce television for a year and to banish from their hearts each anxiety and anguish about the future."[107]

What interesting practical counsel! By turning off the television, the youths would greatly reduce the background noise in their lives (note that this was before the appearance of ubiquitous computers and smartphones) enabling them to hear that still, small voice better. The cardinal said that they found turning off the TV the easier of the two rules, but the second was equally important. When we refuse to distress ourselves over the future, we better submit ourselves to the will of God and the counsel of the Holy Spirit. How often does the command "Be not afraid" appear in Scripture, words of counsel of such great importance. Pope St. John Paul II was known for often repeating this phrase after asking that we listen to God. We'd surely do well to heed those words of counsel.

PRAYING FOR COUNSEL

Sts. Thomas and Bonaventure concur in linking the petition of the Lord's Prayer "Forgive us our trespasses as we forgive those who trespass against us" to the gift of counsel. This connection may not be obvious at first glance, but Thomas has clearly laid it out for us by noting that a person needs counsel when he is in trouble, as he needs to consult a doctor when he is sick.

[106] *The Gifts of the Holy Spirit*, p. 65.
[107] Ibid., p. 66.

So when his soul is sick through sin he must seek counsel in order to be healed. That the sinner needs counsel is indicated in the words of Daniel: "Let my counsel be acceptable unto thee, O King, and redeem thou my sins with alms." Hence, it is a very good counsel against sin that a man give alms and show mercy. For this reason the Holy Spirit teaches sinners to make this petition and to pray, "Forgive us our trespasses."[108]

Indeed, as Thomas's last words suggest, prayer itself can be both an act guided by counsel and a means of petitioning for it. Whenever we are faced with a situation in which our most prudent deliberations can't seem to arrive at the appropriate course of action, it is time to call in the power of prayer. As Fr. Kelly has written so well: "It is in prayer rather than study that we shall come to know the gift of Counsel; for Counsel is a gift of God and only the prayer of God lays bare its secrets."[109]

Let us pray then right now with the petition for the gift of counsel from St. Alphonsus Liguori: "Grant me the spirit of counsel that I may ever choose the surest way of pleasing God and gaining heaven. Amen."

FROM COUNSEL FLOWS MERCY, GOODNESS, AND BENIGNITY

St. Thomas again echoes St. Augustine in explaining how the beatitude of mercy corresponds to the gift of counsel. Per Augustine: "Counsel is befitting the merciful, because the one remedy is to be delivered from evils so great, to pardon, and to

---

[108] *The Aquinas Catechism*, p. 143, citing Daniel 4:4.
[109] *The Seven Gifts*, p. 73.

give."[110] Thomas cites 1 Timothy 4:8, "Godliness is profitable to all things,"[111] and explains that the beatitude of mercy corresponds to the gift of counsel, not because counsel elicits or gives rise to mercy, but because counsel guides and directs how mercy is acted out.

As for the fruits that grow from counsel's tree, Thomas notes that counsel pertains, of course, to practical actions, and these are done with *goodness* and *benignity* (or kindness), as befitting acts of mercy when directed by the gift of counsel.

OUR LADY OF GOOD COUNSEL[112]

The Blessed Mother revealed her receptivity to the counsel of the Holy Spirit when the Angel Gabriel hailed her as full of grace

[110] *ST*, II-II, Q. 53, art.1.

[111] Ibid. And note that the Dominican Fathers explain in their translation that the word *godliness* translates the Latin word *pietas*, from which our English word *pity* derives and which is the same as *mercy*.

[112] Mother Mary has also been intricately associated with "good counsel" and has been given the title Our Lady (or Mother) of Good Counsel for many centuries. Tradition relates a miracle in the year 1467 in which heavenly music was heard and a cloud appeared over an unfinished wall of a church the Augustinians were renovating in Genazzano, Italy. When the cloud lifted, the crowd saw there a fresco, of about one foot by one foot and a half, of the Madonna and Child on a sliver of plaster no thicker than an eggshell. Many miracles were reported thereafter, and the painting became known as Our Lady of Good Counsel. Many popes in the last three centuries were devoted to Our Lady of Good Counsel, including Benedict XIV, who promoted the devotion; Leo XII, who added the title Mother of Good Counsel to the Litany of Loreto; and Pius XII, who dedicated his pontificate to her.

and said to her, "Do not be afraid, Mary, for you have found favor with God" (Luke 1:30). As Mary absorbed the angel's astounding message about the greatest of all honors to be bestowed on her for the benefit of all of humanity, her prudence did not fail to operate. She remembered her pious vow of virginity, applied her reasoning powers to this apparent conflict, and applied caution before answering by asking Gabriel, "How can this be since I have no husband?" She was perfectly docile in learning from the angel the great miracle that would ensue when he told her, "The Holy Spirit will come upon you, and the power of the Most High will overshadow you; therefore the child to be born will be called holy, the Son of God" (Luke 1:35).

Eve, the first woman, had heeded the advice of the most evil and deceptive of counselors, Satan in the guise of a serpent, binding us in sin, but God told the serpent, "I will put enmities between thee and the woman, and thy seed and her seed: she shall crush thy head, and thou shalt lie in wait for her heel" (Gen. 3:15, Douay-Rheims).[113] Mary, the new Eve, heeded the counsel of the Holy Spirit and was God's willing handmaid in bringing to us Christ, who would refuse to heed Satan's counsels

---

[113] Some English translations use *he*, and some use *she*, as do different ancient Hebrew texts, including those cited by the philosopher Philo, the historian Josephus, and the rabbi whom St. Thomas Aquinas held in such esteem, Moses Maimonides. The Latin Vulgate used the feminine pronoun, stressing the importance of the woman earlier in the verse and in salvation history, but either pronoun used is theologically sound, for it is Christ who directly crushes Satan and Mary indirectly as the Mother of God and the new Eve. For an interesting explanation see Dr. Taylor Marshall's article "Who Crushes Satan's Head in Genesis 3:15? (Mary or Jesus?)," http://taylormarshall.com/2010/12/who-crushes-satans-head-in-genesis-315.html.

and would crush him in defeat. And indeed, we'd do well to recall again and heed this woman's famous piece of counsel: "Do whatever he tells you" (John 2:5).

CHRIST COUNSELOR

Christ, of course, was the source of the highest counsel to us during His years on earth, and He clearly made it known that His counsel was not simply to be heard but to be acted upon. It was Christ who declared, "Blessed rather are those who hear the word of God and keep it!" (Luke 11:28) and "If you know these things, blessed are you if you do them" (John 13:17). Christ meant for us to apply His holy principles in all the acts of our daily lives, and He promised to send us a Counselor after Him: "And I will pray to the Father, and he will give you another Counselor, to be with you for ever, even the Spirit of truth, whom the world cannot receive, because it neither sees him nor knows him; you know him, for he dwells with you, and will be in you" (John 14:16–17).

What powerful words of counsel! The world doesn't see the Spirit of truth, but we can if we but choose to look away from the world's distractions and see Him with the eyes of faith. If we cultivate periods of silence away from the din of all the world's false counselors, we will hear His still, small voice, which comes from within us, and then proceed to do whatever He tells us, confident that He is guiding us along the right path to ultimate joy in heaven.

PROFILE IN GIFTEDNESS #5

ST. FRANCIS DE SALES: GOD'S GIFTED COUNSELOR

Recalling St. Thomas's observation that through the Holy Spirit's gift of counsel in addition to His direct guidance, we may also be led to sources of good counsel on earth, I'll opine that for men and women living in our world today, there is hardly any better, more practical counsel to be found than in the writings of St. Francis de Sales (1567–1622).

Francis de Sales lived in the throes of the controversies after the Reformation. Indeed, although he was the bishop of Geneva, he entered the Calvinist-held city only twice in his life! In the year 1604 he met a widow, Jane de Chantal, whom he had seen in a dream, and become her spiritual director. This step led to a life of spiritual direction through countless one-on-one encounters with laymen and -women of the world, not to mention more than twenty thousand letters.[114]

The gift of counsel, as we saw, is a gift that gets things done, being focused on the means of achieving virtuous goals and growing in our union with Christ through the acts of our daily lives. This indeed is where St. Francis excelled. His spiritual classic, *Introduction to the Devout Life*, has been called the greatest Catholic book for laypeople and has guided them for more than four hundred years and in countless editions.[115] So focused was St. Francis on growing holy through the simple acts of daily life

---

[114] No wonder he's a patron saint of writers!

[115] No wonder he's also a patron saint of publishers!

that a most recent distillation of his wisdom for modern readers is entitled *Live Today Well*, drawing upon the saint's words of counsel to "think only of living today well, and when tomorrow comes, it also will be today and we can think of it then."[116]

At a time when some Reformers sought to squelch the simple joys in people's lives, St. Francis's *Introduction* was blasted from some pulpits and ripped to shreds by some preachers, for the saint discussed and tolerated such simple human delights as joking and dancing![117]

Perhaps St. Francis's most basic counsel to us all is to be mindful that, regardless of our worldly occupations and responsibilities, we are all called to grow in and enjoy devout lives dedicated to Christ.

St. Francis de Sales's feast day is January 24.

St. Francis de Sales, pray for us, that, by embracing the gift of counsel of the Holy Spirit, and by drinking deeply of the wise counsel of saints such as you, we too may grow in the devout life, the life of true love of God.

---

[116] Fr. Thomas F. Dailey, O.S.F.S., *Live Today Well: St. Francis de Sales's Simple Approach to Holiness* (Manchester, NH: Sophia Institute Press, 2015), v.

[117] St. Thomas would surely have agreed with the saint in his counsel: "A man who is without mirth, not only is lacking playful speech, but is also burdensome to others, since he is deaf to the moderate mirth of others." *ST*, II-II, Q. 168, art. 4.

ANGELIC ANALYSIS #5
THE SEVEN GIFTS

The gifts are habits perfecting man so that he is ready
to follow the promptings of the Holy Ghost,
even as the moral virtues perfect the appetitive powers so that they obey reason.

—St. Thomas Aquinas, *Summa Theologica*, I-II, Q. 68, art. 5

Question 68 of the *Summa Theologica*, "Of the Gifts," is St.
Thomas's first explicit treatment of the seven gifts of the Holy
Spirit. The question comprises eight articles, each beginning with
a question that can be answered yes or no. Of course, St. Thomas's
treatment goes far beyond just that one word that matters so
much, but for brevity's sake we will cut to the chase and provide
just the gist of his answer. The philosophically and theologically
inclined are invited to delve into the *Summa* itself if my sum-
maries seem insufficient.

As to this first question, whether the gifts differ from the
virtues, Thomas answers yes (which indeed is the answer to all
of these questions) and explains the differences. He notes that
Scripture, when referring to what we have come to call the gifts,
uses the word *spiritus*[118] (spirit) rather than *gift*.[119] The word *spirit*

---

[118] In the Latin translation Thomas used, based upon St. Jerome's
Vulgate.
[119] To refresh our memories here with the RSV translation: "And
the Spirit of the LORD shall rest upon him, the spirit of wisdom
and understanding, the spirit of counsel and might, the spirit

denotes that these gifts are given to us as spirits or breathings, through divine inspiration. They are a motion from outside and above us. So here is the crux of the difference:

> Now it is manifest that human virtues perfect man according as it is natural for him to be moved by his reason in his interior and exterior actions. Consequently man needs yet higher perfections, whereby to be disposed to be moved by God. These perfections are called gifts, not only because they are infused by God, but also because by them man is disposed to become amenable to Divine inspiration.

Despite their similarities, then, there are fundamental differences between virtues and gifts. The virtues, even the infused theological virtues given to us by God, are used as guided by our human reasoning faculties, whereas the seven gifts make us open in our thoughts and actions to the stirrings of the Holy Spirit.

MUST WE HAVE THE GIFTS TO BE SAVED?

St. Thomas says that we need the gifts to be saved. He notes, "It is written (Wis. 7:28): *God loveth no one but him that dwelleth with wisdom*; and of fear (Sirach 1:28): *He that is without fear cannot be justified*." He argues that as wisdom, the highest of the gifts, and fear, the lowest, are necessary, so too are all the gifts placed between them. He notes that virtues born of or guided by reason alone are not enough to lead us to heaven without

---

of knowledge and the fear of the Lord. And his delight shall be in the fear of the LORD" (Isa. 11:2–3).

the assistance of the promptings of the Holy Spirit, according to Romans 8:14:

> *Whosoever are led by the Spirit of God, they are the sons of God ... and if sons, heirs, also*: and ... *Thy good Spirit shall lead me into the right land*, because, to wit, none can receive the blessed inheritance of that land of the blessed, except he be moved and led thither by the Holy Ghost. Therefore, in order to accomplish this end, it is necessary for man to have the gift of the Holy Ghost.

ARE THE GIFTS HABITS?

The gifts are indeed habits, and here they share similarities with the virtues. Habits are firm dispositions to act in certain ways, and virtues, as we have seen, are essentially good habits. The gifts too are good habits, dispositions toward good actions, although under the guidance of the Holy Spirit rather than human reason. "Therefore, the gifts of the Holy Ghost are habits whereby man is perfected to obey readily the Holy Ghost."

IS SEVEN THE RIGHT NUMBER OF GIFTS?

St. Thomas says that the seven gifts are "suitably enumerated." As virtues perfect man's powers as moved "by the command of reason," the gifts perfect man's powers as "moved by the instinct of God." Therefore, whatever human powers can be perfected by virtues attain even higher perfection through the assistance of the gifts. Please refer to this book's appendices for a table that fleshes this out for each human power, action, and gift.

DO THE GIFTS HANG TOGETHER?

St. Thomas proceeds to tell us that the gifts are all interconnected. He begins at the allegorical level by quoting from St. Gregory's *Moralia*: "It is worthy to note in this feast of Job's sons, that by turns they fed one another. Now the sons of Job, of whom he is speaking, denote the gifts of the Holy Ghost. Therefore the gifts of the Holy Ghost are connected together by strengthening one another." He then notes that the Holy Spirit dwells within us by charity, "according to Rom. 5:5: *The charity of God is poured forth in our hearts by the Holy Ghost, Who is given to us.*" So, just as the virtues are united and guided by prudence, so too are the gifts of the Holy Spirit "connected together in charity; so that whoever has charity has all the gifts of the Holy Ghost, none of which one can possess without charity." According to St. Thomas, the gifts of the Holy Spirit flow from the virtue of charity and serve it.

DO THE GIFTS REMAIN IN HEAVEN?

St. Thomas begins with a powerful citation of St. Ambrose: "The city of God, the heavenly Jerusalem is not washed with the waters of an earthly river: it is the Holy Ghost, of Whose outpouring we but taste, Who proceeding from the Fount of life, seems to flow more abundantly in those celestial spirits, a seething torrent of sevenfold heavenly virtue." (Can you even begin to imagine the sight of such a "seething torrent of sevenfold heavenly virtue," perhaps but one of the countless wonders awaiting us through the eternal beatific vision the gifts can help us attain?) Thomas elaborates that while on earth the gifts make the mind amenable to the prompting of the Holy Spirit, this will be "especially realized in heaven, where God will be *all in all* (1 Cor. 15:28)." The gifts will no longer be addressed to earthly concerns, but solely to matters divine.

ARE SOME GIFTS GREATER THAN OTHERS?

St. Thomas agrees with St. Augustine's observation that Isaiah lists these gifts in order from the greatest to the least. He enumerates wisdom and understanding first, which are greater excellences because they perfect the highest powers of the speculative intellect; next counsel and fortitude because they deal with especially difficult matters; knowledge and piety, dealing with more ordinary matters follow; and fear is the last and the least, but it serves as the foundation and beginning of all the others.

VIRTUES VERSUS GIFTS: WHICH ONES WIN?

If you have followed the last of St. Thomas's questions and answers, you might expect (and rightly so), that the gifts are superior to the natural virtues, both moral and intellectual, since the virtues struggle under the guidance of limited human reason, while the gifts sail forth as moved by the motions of the Holy Spirit. But what does St. Thomas make of the theological virtues of faith, hope, and charity? These supernatural virtues are infused in our souls by God, as, indeed, are the gifts. The supernatural virtues are still subject to the workings of human reason, which suggests their inferiority to the gifts in that regard, but Thomas notes that as the intellectual virtues are more perfect than the moral virtues and regulate or control them because of their direct ties to the human intellect rather than our animal appetite, so too are the theological virtues actually more perfect than the gifts of the Holy Spirit and regulate or control them.

Moving to the fascinating allegories of Gregory, Thomas cites from the *Moralia on Job* that "the seven sons, i.e., the seven gifts, never attain the perfection of the number ten, unless all that they do be done in faith, hope, and charity." Indeed, of all the virtues and the gifts, as St. Paul notes, the greatest of these is charity. It is that great theological virtue that "quickens" or makes alive and makes possible the gifts of the Holy Spirit.

The goal of charity is union with God, the object of its love. Such union in heaven will provide eternal bliss in the beatific vision, and even on earth the theological virtues and the gifts of the Holy Spirit may provide a foretaste of such blessedness that we have come to call the Beatitudes.

THE MANY GIFTS OF POPE ST. GREGORY THE GREAT

Pope St. Gregory the Great (540–604) was the second pope in history to be labeled "the Great," the first being Pope St. Leo the Great (ca. 400–461).[120] Gregory held the post of an important government official in Rome before converting to Christ and converting his palace into a monastery. A deep thinker by nature and a contemplative hermit by choice, he heeded the Holy Spirit's call to the papacy, earning the title "the Great" by feats such as extending the presence of the Church into new lands, including England. (He famously said of the fair youths of that land that rather than Angles, they should be called angels!)

Gregory, along with Jerome, another of the four original Latin Church Doctors, also had a great impact on future theologians through his magnificent writings, in particular his *Moralia on the Book of Job* that would so profoundly influence St. Thomas Aquinas in his own further explication of both the seven deadly sins and the seven gifts of the Holy Spirit. As for the gifts, we saw that Gregory explained that the seven sons of Job represent the seven gifts and that the way they fed each other represents the way the gifts are connected and support one another.

---

[120] Leo was a champion of Christ's Incarnation and divine and human natures and was famous for persuading Attila the Hun to turn his army away from the walls of Rome. As for Gregory's own greatness, it was this great pope who coined the most humble papal title of "Servant of the servants of God."

As a pope, Gregory honestly lamented the loss of his contemplative life, writing, "but now, by reason of my pastoral charge, my poor soul is forced to endure the burden of secular men's business, and after so sweet a kind of rest."[121] Nonetheless, St. Gregory followed wherever the Spirit led him, and even today we can enjoy the gifts he left for us in his writings and his influence.

Pope St. Gregory's feast day is September 8.

Pope St. Gregory, pray for us, that we may share our gifts with others in whatever station God calls us to in life.

---

[121] Edmund C. Gardner, ed., *The Dialogues of Saint Gregory the Great* (Merchantville, NJ: Evolution Press, 2010), p. 4.

CHAPTER 6

UNWRAPPING UNDERSTANDING

Understanding denotes a certain excellence of a knowledge that penetrates into the heart of things.

—St. Thomas Aquinas, *Summa Theologica*, II-II, Q. 8, art. 1.

It is the rule of moral definition, the door to learned
thought, and the key to heavenly contemplation. And such understanding is indeed a gift.

—St. Bonaventure, *Collations*

UNDERSTANDING ... UNDERSTANDING

The human capacity to understand and the intellectual virtue of understanding that perfects it are in themselves natural gifts from God of the very highest importance. Understanding is one of the fundamental ways through which we are elevated above all other species of living beings on earth and in which we were made in the image and likeness of God. St. Thomas tells us, "The nature of each thing is shown by its operation. Now, the proper operation of man is to understand; because he thereby surpasses all other animals."[122] In other words, we are the only species on earth that is capable of true understanding. So, what is this thing that you, my reader can do, that your dog or your cat could not begin to understand?

In a nutshell, the virtue of science relates to the grasp of cause-and-effect relationships, while understanding pertains to the comprehension of fundamental and overarching principles. Let's get a little closer to the heart of the matter by repeating St.

---

[122] *ST*, I, Q. 76, art. 1. For a detailed summary of Thomas's analysis of the nature of the human capacity of understanding and how it builds upon both the five external senses and the four internal senses, see chapter 1, "Understanding ... Understanding," in my *Unearthing Your Ten Talents* or, for a brief version, chapter 3, "What Does a Soul Do?" in my *One-Minute Aquinas*.

Thomas's pithy quotation with which we started this chapter: "Understanding denotes a certain excellence of a knowledge that penetrates into the heart of things." Understanding, per Thomas, implies an "intimate knowledge, for *intelligere* (to understand) is the same as *intus legere* (to read inwardly). This is clear to anyone who considers the difference between intellect and sense, because sensitive knowledge is concerned with sensible qualities, whereas intellective knowledge penetrates into the very essence of a thing."[123]

Our dogs and cats have the same five senses that we do (in fact, their senses of hearing and smell are more acute than ours), yet they cannot grasp the heart of things, fundamental essences and underlying principles. Dogs and cats can see and interact with other sensible, individual dogs and cats, but they cannot grasp the concept of "dogness" or "catness," let alone talk about, write about, or argue with each other about such things. It is through the powers of human understanding that we can penetrate to the essence, the *quiddity*, the "whatness" that makes a thing the kind of thing that it is. And our powers of understanding are not limited to small furry creatures or to any objects of the senses at all, because we can also come to understand to some extent the essence of important abstract concepts, such as truth, virtue, or indeed, the gifts of the Holy Spirit.

Our powers of understanding begin with self-evident principles, such as Aristotle's law of noncontradiction in logic, that "one cannot say of something that it is and that it is not in the same respect and at the same time." Ethical principles guiding human conduct include the precepts "Do the good" and "Avoid

---

[123] *ST*, II-II, Q. 8, art. 1.

the evil." These kinds of fundamental principles are the starting points for all the kinds of detailed chains of reasoning that take place when we employ the intellectual virtues of science and wisdom.

So, with that extremely brief primer on the nature of natural understanding, let's jump in to understanding as a gift of the Holy Spirit that brings us yet closer to the God in whose image and likeness we were made.

THE PENETRATING LIGHT OF THE HOLY SPIRIT

St. Thomas reports that understanding flows from the infused virtue of faith and proceeds to perfect it with deeper penetration and a confident sense of certainty in belief. St. Gregory, he notes, has stated that "understanding enlightens the mind concerning the things it has heard."[124] In his treatment of the gift of understanding, the Seraphic Bonaventure cites Daniel 2:21–22: "He gives wisdom to the wise and knowledge to those who have understanding; he reveals deep and mysterious things; he knows what is in the darkness, and the light dwells within him."[125]

Still, while sojourning here on earth we can never completely understand the mysteries of God, but the gift of understanding can help us better grasp even this limitation. It can make us more aware of God's unfathomable awesomeness. Please allow me to offer this simple analogy. Imagine you are in a pitch-dark room and in one corner lies a bottomless pit, or perhaps a black hole. (We assume for our purposes that the black hole has not sucked you in!) Surrounded by darkness, you have no clue that

[124] *ST*, II-II, Q. 8, art. 3.
[125] *Collations*, p. 173.

the pit is there. Now imagine that you have been given a very powerful flashlight. Scanning the room, you now become aware of this fascinating, mysterious phenomenon. There it is! And yet, when you shine your light into the pit, the light does not have the power to penetrate fully "into its heart" and show you just what it is. The pit remains mysterious and unfathomable, yet now you understand that it certainly exists, that it is right there with you, and that its awesome mystery exceeds your powers of full comprehension.

The gift of understanding is like a powerful supernatural light that illuminates our capacity to know God through faith and reason, to know that He is there even in our darkest hours and to help us understand the very limits of our understanding. Of course, God is not too *dark* to fathom. On the contrary, His light is too bright for the eyes we have now, but just wait for that glorified body with eyes that will behold God in the beatific vision! While the essence of God Himself exceeds the power of our light of understanding, the penetration that the Holy Spirit's gift of understanding provides for us can help us on our way toward that face-to-face meeting when we'll see God more clearly than ever before.

The gift of understanding, although most lofty, abstract, and speculative, has practical uses as well. Thomas notes that "'*faith worketh through charity*,' according to the Apostle (Gal. 5:6)."[126] Faith works, understanding perfects faith through the stirrings of the Holy Spirit, and therefore, understanding also works: it works to guide our actions to a deeper understanding of the principles of God's eternal law. Indeed, "the eternal law surpasses human reason; so that the knowledge of human actions, as ruled by the

[126] Ibid., art. 3.

eternal law, surpasses the natural reason, and requires the super-natural light of a gift of the Holy Ghost."[127]

UNDERSTANDING THE SACRAMENTS

Truly then, understanding is among the most outstanding gifts that the Holy Spirit has given us. So how might we use the sacraments Christ gave us to grow in the use of this gift? Like the other gifts, understanding is bestowed in its primitive form in the sacrament of Baptism. It is strengthened at Confirmation, and the timing is very appropriate: Baptism is most often conferred in infancy, although an infant is not able to understand the language and significance of the rite. A school-aged child, a teen, or an adult, however, has developed the language and reasoning capacities to understand the language and the significance of the Confirmation rite.

Of course, if we are to be open to the Holy Spirit's guidance in understanding the truths of the Faith at deeper levels, we must remember that we have been graced with such a gift. We must make an effort to apply our natural powers of understanding to growing in our comprehension of the things of the Faith, including the sacraments, not only by receiving them but through spiritual reading and contemplation.[128] Thomas has told us that since "grace does not destroy nature, but perfects it, natural reason

[127] Ibid.
[128] We should especially apply our understanding to the greatest sacrament: the Eucharist. Thomas notes that understanding penetrates truths that remain hidden to the senses, as he has expressed most beautifully in his Prayer *Laude Sion Salvatorem* (Praise, O Zion, thy Savior) for the feast of Corpus Christi (the Body and Blood of Christ): "Look! upon the altar lies, hidden

should minister to the faith as the natural bent of the will minis-
ters to charity."[129] It's our job to use our natural thinking capacities
to give that gift of grace something to build upon!

IS HEBETUDE OF THE SENSES DULLING YOUR UNDERSTANDING?

We saw that *ignorance* was a vice directly opposed to the gift
of knowledge because it represents a lack of effort to know the
things of the Faith that we should know. Now, *hebetude* is a word
we don't hear too often these days. It derives from the Latin word
hebes, which means "blunt" or "dull." When we fail to employ
our capacity for understanding, our minds — the greatest and
potentially sharpest implements God has given us — become
blunt, dull, and unable to "penetrate into the heart of things."
We render ourselves spiritual dullards when we live our lives
at the level of the pleasures of the sense without engaging our
intellects to think about deeper and higher things. We fail to
achieve our spiritual potential when we live too much on the
plane of the animal. We fail to feed our intellects when we feed
only our senses.

If we want to employ our powers of understanding so that they
may be perfected by the Holy Spirit's gift, we need to sharpen
the blades of our minds by penetrating into the things of the
Faith, focusing less on our pop culture of death and more on the
Church's culture of life, spending less time learning about the lives
of criminals or celebrities (which are too often one and the same)
and more time learning about the lives of the saints.

---

deep from human eyes, bread of angels from the skies, made
the food of mortal man."

[129] *ST*, I, Q. 1, art. 8.

St. Bonaventure notes other ways we can hinder or foster growth in the gift of understanding. He starts with some verses from the Psalms: "I will bless the Lord who has given me understanding" (see Ps. 15:7, Douay-Rheims) and "The declaration of your words illumines, and gives understanding to the little ones" (see Ps. 118:130, Douay-Rheims). Further, regarding Christ's saying, "You have hidden these things from the wise and the prudent and revealed them to the little ones" (see Matt. 11:25), St. Bonaventure explains that the little ones are those who are *humble* and that "nothing darkens the understanding about matters that pertain to God as much as does presumption."[130] The person who presumes that he already knows it all is not in a position to submit to the Holy Spirit to receive the gift of understanding! Indeed, St. Bonaventure elaborates the point later, citing the kind of verbal outspokenness and imprudence that flows from such presumption: "It is written in Sirach 5:14: 'If you have understanding, answer your neighbor; if not, put your hand over your mouth.'"

In addition to the humility that wards off presumption, Bonaventure highlights that *ingratitude* can block the flow of understanding, recalling how King David blessed God for his gift of understanding. Indeed, we should feel and express gratitude for every one of the gifts, thereby disposing ourselves to receive and utilize each gift best.

PRAYER: AN ACT OF THE INTELLECT

St. Thomas notes that prayer itself is a powerful act of the intellect possible only to man among all of the creatures on earth.

---

[130] *Collations*, p. 161.

"According to Cassiodorus, *prayer* (oratio) *is spoken reason* (oris ratio)."[131] Speech is a function of the intellect, so prayer is an act not of the lower, sensitive powers, but of the intellectual powers unique to humans. Thomas explains that prayer starts with and is essentially "the raising up of one's mind to God"[132] and that the "parts" of prayer include *supplications* (humble requests) for particular blessings from God (including the gifts!) and *thanksgivings* (thus showing gratitude) for the blessings He has already provided.

As for the prayer the Lord Himself gave us, the Seraphic Doctor links the sixth petition, "and lead us not into temptation," with the gift of understanding. It is those temptations of the world, after all, that lead to hebetude of the senses, that dullness of the capacity of our intellects to penetrate into the heart of truths that really matter. Indeed, this point will be made more sharply below when the Angelic Doctor chimes in about understanding's beatitude. Let us pray with St. Alphonsus Liguori: "Grant me the spirit of understanding to enlighten my mind with the light of Thy divine truth."

THE PURE OF HEART UNDERSTAND

St. Thomas cites St. Augustine as follows: "The sixth work of the Holy Ghost which is understanding, is applicable to the clean of heart, whose eye being purified, they can see what eye hath not seen."[133] Thomas goes on to explain a "twofold" kind of cleanness of heart. The first is a cleansing of inappropriate affections

---

[131] *ST*, II-II, Q. 83, art. 17.
[132] Ibid.
[133] *ST*, II-II, Q. 8, art. 7.

for things of the world that is produced by the virtues and gifts "belonging to the appetitive power."[134] The other cleansing "is a kind of complement to the sight of God," in which the mind is purged of sense-based images and of intellectual errors, so that we may rise above sense-based images to a higher view of God and avoid the misrepresentations promoted by heresies against the truths of the Church. Further, there are two ways in which we see God:

1. imperfectly on earth, where we cannot see His essence but can see what He is *not*, thereby deepening our understanding of how He surpasses human understanding

2. perfectly in heaven, where, in the state of perfection, God will reveal to us His essence, thereby producing the unimaginable bliss of the beatific vision

I can't help but observe that both St. Thomas and St. Bonaventure were blessed in an extraordinary way on earth with their gifts of understanding, no doubt because they so purified their hearts, turning their eyes from the things of creation to focus their vision upon the Creator.

And as for the fruits that flow from understanding, Thomas addresses the paradox that while the gift of understanding *flows from* the theological virtue of faith, faith is also its end or its fruit. St. Thomas's insight in unraveling this spiritual conundrum comes from a gloss[135] on Galatians 5:22 that says "faith

---

[134] Ibid. For example, temperance, fortitude, and justice among the virtues, and fear, fortitude, and piety among the gifts.

[135] The *Glossa Ordinaria* Thomas often refers to was a widely used medieval commentary on all the texts of the Bible, pulling primarily from the writings of the early Church Fathers. Thomas would later go on to compose his own *catena aurea* (golden

which is a fruit, is certitude about the unseen."[136] Therefore, the fruit of faith that derives from the gift of understanding is that special *certitude* and confidence about the things a person believes through faith. This experience of certitude is much more gratifying than doubt, so it also contributes to the experience of the fruit of *joy*.

MOTHER MARY'S UNEARTHLY UNDERSTANDING

When Fr. Formby looked at how the Blessed Mother modeled the gift of the spirit of understanding, he harked back to some of the oldest books of Jewish Scripture, where, in Exodus and Deuteronomy, God gave Moses the Ten Commandments. Fr. Formby highlighted the third, whereby we keep holy the Sabbath Day. Although we toil for our livelihood up to six days a week, that seventh day was to be set aside to contemplate and honor the Divine Creator. It was a day set aside to grow in our understanding, in part through the study of Sacred Scripture. Fr. Formby notes that the evangelists who wrote the four Gospels did not explicitly tell us what a typical Sabbath Day might have been within the Holy Family, but he gathers plenty of evidence that Mary must have spent that day helping herself and her family grow in understanding of the ways of the Lord. Although the words of her great Magnificat were inspired by the Holy Spirit, they built upon her understanding derived from sacred study. When she exclaimed, "He has put down the mighty from their thrones and exalted those of low degree" (Luke 1:52), for example, she echoed the

---

chain) of commentaries on the Gospels from both Greek and Latin Fathers.

[136] *ST*, II-II, Q. 8, art. 8.

words that the Lord spoke to King Nebuchadnezzar before he drove him away: "the Most High rules the kingdoms of men and gives it to whom he will" (Dan. 4:17).

Further, pay heed to Mary's zeal for understanding when the shepherds came into Bethlehem and told of the wondrous things an angel of the Lord had told them about the birth of Christ the Lord. While the inhabitants "wondered at what the shepherds told them … Mary kept all these things, pondering them in her heart" (Luke 2:18, 19) striving for deeper levels of understanding to penetrate into the heart of those things. When Mary and Joseph found the child Jesus in the Temple, He said to them, "'Did you not know that I must be in my Father's house?' And they did not understand the saying which he spoke to them" (Luke 2:49–50). Yet it was noted specifically of Mary that regarding Jesus' deeds and words of that day, "his mother kept all these things in her heart" (Luke 2:51). She would not be satisfied until she could understand. We too should ponder Christ's teachings as Mary did, treasuring them in our hearts.

BURNING WITH UNDERSTANDING ON THE ROAD TO EMMAUS

In treating of the relationship between faith and the gift of the spirit of understanding, St. Thomas wrote that "Our Lord opened the scriptures to His disciples, that they might understand them. Therefore, understanding is compatible with the faith."[137]

In the amazing scriptural account to which St. Thomas refers, we find Cleopas and another disciple sharing their faith with an apparent stranger, telling the then-brand-new story of Christ's

---

[137] *ST*, II-II, Q. 8, art. 2, referencing Luke 24:27, 32.

death and glorious Resurrection, "but their eyes were kept from recognizing him" (Luke 24:16), so they did not know at first that the man they journeyed with as they walked toward the village of Emmaus was the risen Christ Himself! Christ then began to open up the Scriptures for them, explaining how Moses and the prophets had said so many things concerning His life, death, and Resurrection. Relishing the stranger's company and His great depth of understanding, they invited Him to stay and eat supper with them. Then, "when he was at table with them, he took the bread and blessed, and broke it, and gave it to them" (Luke 24:30) — words we know so well from the Mass. It was then that they saw, through the eyes of faith, what had been hidden to their earthly eyes. They recognized that the stranger to whom they spoke about Christ *was* the Lord Jesus Christ! At the moment of their realization, though, He disappeared from their sight. In their amazement they recalled to one another how their "hearts burned" as Jesus had opened the Scriptures to them.

When Jesus appeared to His apostles soon after, they were frightened and confused, but Jesus showed them the wounds of His hands and feet and even ate some broiled fish to show them that He was no disembodied spirit, but Jesus returned in the flesh. Again, "he opened their minds to the scriptures," proclaiming His death and Resurrection "and that repentance and forgiveness of sins should be preached in his name to all nations" (Luke 24:47).

If we are to surrender to the Holy Spirit so that His gift of understanding might open our minds and set aflame our hearts, we would do well to ponder prayerfully Christ's life in the Gospels and to receive regularly the Real Presence of His body, blood, soul, and divinity in the Eucharist He has provided to give us eternal life.

THE SERAPHIC DOCTOR
SEES AND UNDERSTANDS

In the past, when writing about virtues and about the Dominican Order, I have offered Sts. Augustine of Hippo and Catherine of Siena as models of understanding. Augustine, after all, is, along with St. Thomas Aquinas, a pillar of the Catholic Church, as may be seen by Thomas's almost countless references to him, and the *Catechism*'s almost countless references to both of them. Further, it was Augustine who argued that the three primary powers of the human soul— memory, understanding, and will—mirror, in a dim way, the Holy Trinity. As for St. Catherine of Siena, we know that "understanding penetrates into the heart of things," and that "the pure of heart shall see God." She was blessed with many visions of God, and in one mystical experience Christ even exchanged his heart with hers. Catherine has been called the Seraphic Virgin, since the seraphs look upon God. For our purposes here in this book, what better saintly model could we use for the gift of understanding, then, than the "Seraphic Doctor," St. Bonaventure?

St. Bonaventure (1221–1274), was St. Thomas's almost exact contemporary, and we have seen glimpses of just how well the great Franciscan understood all the gifts of the Holy Spirit—indeed, *through* those very gifts grafted onto a lifetime of saintly study. While the two great saints differed at times in matters of philosophy, they shared in their theologies and in their saintly lives a passion to understand and penetrate into the heart of the things of God, including, of course, His great gifts. St. Bonaventure used his God-given sanctifying and gratuitous graces to lead us all to a deeper understanding of things of the Faith through his voluminous writings on theological and spiritual matters, as well as in a biography of his order's founder, St. Francis of Assisi (1182–1226). The world lost the Seraphic Doctor on July 15, 1274, only four months after the Angelic Doctor rose to heaven.

St. Bonaventure's feast day is July 15.

> *St. Bonaventure, pray for us, that through the*
> *Holy Spirit's gift of understanding, we may*
> *penetrate into the heart of the things that matter most*
> *and come to see and share the heart of Jesus Christ.*

ANGELIC ANALYSIS #6

THE GIFTS AND THE BEATITUDES

Blessed are the poor in spirit, for theirs is the kingdom of
heaven.
Blessed are those who mourn, for they shall be comforted.
Blessed are the meek, for they shall inherit the earth.
Blessed are those who hunger and thirst for righteousness, for
they shall be satisfied.
Blessed are the merciful, for they shall obtain mercy.
Blessed are the pure in heart, for they shall see God.
Blessed are the peacemakers, for they shall be called sons of
God.
Blessed are those who are persecuted for righteousness'
sake, for theirs is the kingdom of heaven.

—Matthew 5:3–10

Certain things are included among the beatitudes that are neither virtues nor gifts, e.g. poverty, mourning, and peace. Therefore, the beatitudes differ from the virtues and the gifts.

—St. Thomas Aquinas, *Summa Theologica*, I-II, Q. 69, art. 2

St. Thomas devotes four articles in question 69 of the first part
of the second part of the *Summa Theologica* to an examination
of the beatitudes, examining issues such as what he called the
"merits," and the "rewards" of each beatitude, whether they are
numbered correctly, and whether they pertain only to our life
on earth or also to life in heaven. To serve our gift-centered
focus in this brief analysis, I will simply address St. Thomas's

first article, "Whether the Beatitudes Differ from the Virtues and Gifts," and then provide a sneak peek at just which beatitudes flow from each gift (along with a small free gift — a table that sums it all up!).

So then, to determine whether beatitudes differ from gifts, since we've already looked at just what the gifts are, it's time to zoom in on these eight special blessings described most fully by Christ in His Sermon on the Mount.[138] Thomas notes that each beatitude involves a *merit*, an *act* prompted by the virtues and gifts that leads to a specific *reward*, a state of imperfect happiness in this life or perfect happiness in the next that flows from those meritorious behaviors prompted by the virtues and the gifts. Regarding differences between the beatitudes, the gifts, and the virtues, Thomas notes that Sts. "Augustine and Ambrose assign the beatitudes to the gifts and virtues, as *acts* are ascribed to *habits*."[139]

In the beatitudes then, Jesus shows us the kinds of blessed states of happiness that God provides to reward those who act virtuously, although Thomas notes, according to St. John Chrysostom, "all these rewards are one in reality, viz. eternal happiness, which the human intellect cannot grasp. Hence it was necessary to describe it by means of various boons known to us, while observing due proportion to the merits to which those rewards are assigned." So beatitudes are blessed rewards that we would

---

[138] Luke 6:20–22 offers a briefer version, detailing only four of the Beatitudes, that was delivered to the multitude when Jesus came down from a mountain after praying with His disciples. The full rendering Jesus delivered on the mountain to His disciples is found in Matthew 5:3–10, the verses we used to open this chapter.

[139] Emphasis added, with *acts* referring to beatitudes and *habits* to virtues and gifts.

do well to act to obtain. In what ways might the gifts of the Holy Spirit help us to obtain them?

WHICH BEATITUDES FLOW FROM WHICH GIFTS?

Some of this material is provided within our chapters on the individual gifts, so I'll simply provide the table here. You might want to ponder a bit about what Thomas saw as their critical connections. I'll note too that sometimes Thomas mentioned ways in which more than one beatitude was related to a gift. Also, regarding the fact that there are seven gifts, but eight beatitudes, Thomas concludes that the eighth beatitude, "blessed are those who are persecuted for righteousness' sake, for theirs is the kingdom of heaven," is a "confirmation and declaration of all those that precede," a summary of sorts that all the beatitudes produce.

THE BEATITUDES THAT FLOW FROM THE GIFTS

GIFT	BEATITUDE
Fear of the Lord	Poverty of spirit
Piety	Hunger for righteousness Mercifulness
Knowledge	Mourning
Fortitude	Meekness Bearing persecution

THE SEVEN GIFTS OF THE HOLY SPIRIT

GIFT	BEATITUDE
Counsel	Mourning
Understanding	Purity of heart
Wisdom	Peacemaking

The gifts of the Holy Spirit themselves flow from the virtue of charity, and the waters of the virtues and of the gifts nourish and refresh the soul, producing, in addition to the beatitudes, the most holy and succulent fruits. We will harvest the spiritual lessons from this orchard of spiritual fruits in our last Angelic Analysis and Profile in Grace at the end of chapter 7.

BEATITUDES MAN: BLESSED PIER GIORGIO FRASSATI

You don't have to take my word for it that Blessed Pier Giorgio Frassati (1901–1925) was "the man of the eight beatitudes." Pope Saint John Paul II said so on March 27, 1977, while touring an exhibition of photographs of the young man in Krakow, Poland. Thirteen years later, on May 20, 1990, John Paul II beatified the man of the beatitudes in St. Peter's Square.

We saw that St. Brigid, truly a woman of the eight Beatitudes, chose *mercy* as the one dearest to her heart. If Blessed Pier Giorgio were to choose one for his motto, although an argument could be made for any of the eight, *poverty of spirit* seems the most likely candidate. He was born into a wealthy family in Turin, his father the founder and owner of the still extant newspaper *La Stampa*, but Pier Giorgio's heart always went out to the poor—and his feet and the rest of him always followed his heart! He spoke of seeing a special light around the poor, and in one of the earliest of his sister's recollections of their childhood, when young Pier Giorgio once answered a knock at their front door and saw a poor woman holding a child without shoes, he promptly took off his own, gave them to him, and slammed the door so that his parents could not see what he had done!

Throughout his young life he saved his allowance and collected things to sell so that he could give his savings and profits to people in need, whom he sought out in poor neighborhoods. He often arrived to meetings and events covered in sweat, having ridden his bike to save the train fare, and when forced to ride the train to faraway events, he always rode third class. Indeed, his sister reported that when he was asked why he did that, he responded, "Because there is no fourth class." Not only did Blessed Pier Giorgio contribute continuously in such one-on-one acts of mercy toward the poor, but he also became involved in political activities to advocate for the needs of the poor and for fair treatment from those blessed with plenty.

It appears that Pier Giorgio's love for the poor led to his early departure from earth and early arrival in heaven, for he contracted a rare, fatal form of poliomyelitis, most likely from visiting the sick in poverty-stricken districts. Persevering in the beatitude of poverty until his life's end, when he knew his hours on earth were numbered, he handed this note to a friend from the St. Vincent DePaul society: "The injections are for Converso and the pawn ticket belongs to Sappa; I had forgotten it. Please renew it on my account."[140]

Blessed Pier Giorgio Frassati's feast day is the Fourth of July.

Blessed Pier Giorgio, pray for us, that we
too may share our gifts as Christ has instructed
and become men and women of the Beatitudes.

---

[140] Luciana Frassati, *A Man of the Beatitudes: Pier Giorgio Frassati* (San Francisco: Ignatius Press, 2001), p. 151.

CHAPTER 7

WELCOMING WISDOM

It is written (Sirach 6:23): "The wisdom of doctrine is according to her name," for wisdom (*sapientia*) may be described as sweet-tasting science (*sapida scientia*).

—St. Thomas Aquinas, *Summa Theologica*, II-II, Q. 45, art. 4

O taste and see that the LORD is good!

—Psalm 34:8

THE GIFT AT THE TOP OF THE STAIRWAY TO HEAVEN

We've seen how the fear of the Lord is the beginning of wisdom, and how piety, knowledge, fortitude, counsel, and understanding carry us along our way to complete the journey toward wisdom itself, a journey so well worth taking, since "God loves nothing so much as the man who lives in wisdom. For she is more beautiful than the sun, and exceeds every constellation of the stars" (Wisd. 7:28–29). Indeed, the Holy Spirit's gift of wisdom can help us sail beyond the stars, all the way to heaven.

So the Spirit's gift of wisdom is clearly immensely valuable and beautiful to boot, but what exactly is it? Recall, if you will, from chapter 4, that the *virtue* of wisdom was the highest of the three intellectual virtues. St. Thomas sums up their relationship like this:

> Science depends on understanding as on a virtue of higher degree; and both of these depend on wisdom, as claiming the highest place, and containing beneath itself understanding and science, by judging both the conclusions of science, and of the principles on which they are based.[141]

The virtue of *understanding*, you will recall, is based upon our intuitive grasp of self-evident principles and allows us to abstract

[141] *ST*, Q. 57, art. 2.

and form concepts about the singular particular things we encounter through our senses, helping us to "penetrate into the heart of things," to understand the essence or gist of what things are. The virtue of *science*, or *knowledge*, you will recall, is involved in cause-and-effect relationships, and particularly lower or more immediate causes perceptible or deducible from the senses. New principles may emerge from the workings of physical sciences and come to be known as scientific "laws." As for wisdom, above and beyond the knowledge of science, these laws of formal science examine *physical* causes and effects, while the field within philosophy that Aristotle termed *metaphysics*[142] examines the fundamental causes that underlie them, including that ultimate cause of all effects (and all subsequent causes as well), that Uncaused Cause that he called God. This is why Aristotle called metaphysics the "divine science":

> The most divine science is also most honorable; and this science alone is, in two ways, most divine. For the science which it would be most meet for God to have is a divine science, and so is any science that deals with divine objects; and this science alone has both these qualities.... Such a science either God alone can have, or God above all others.[143]

The virtue of *wisdom* then, is a special kind of knowledge that judges of the highest and most fundamental of all causes, a science that studies God, a science worthy of God, and one that only God can fully grasp. Aristotle's most powerful capacities

---

[142] *Meta* (beyond, upon, or transcending) and *physika* (physics or nature).

[143] Aristotle's *Metaphysics*, bk. 1, chap. 2.

for reason could carry even him just so far, though. Aristotle lived three centuries before Christ, and he did not know of the Holy Spirit's *gift of wisdom* described in the Holy Scriptures. The Philosopher's most astute student across the centuries knew it, though, and indeed he possessed it in superabundance, so now let's turn to his explanation.

THE KNOWLEDGE AND WISDOM OF ST. THOMAS AQUINAS (AND OF STS. MATTHEW AND JOHN)

While the gift of knowledge judges primarily of lower, earthly, and human things, it can move us toward the consideration of the higher things of God, but only indirectly, considering how these earthly effects derive from higher causes. "The gift of wisdom," on the other hand, per twentieth-century Thomist Fr. Réginald Garrigou-Lagrange, "proceeds in the opposite direction. It judges first of divine things, then of created things as insets of the divine."[144] In a fascinating insight, Fr. Garrigou-Lagrange observes that the Gospel of St. Matthew may be seen to follow the path of the gift of knowledge in preaching Christ, starting with Christ's human genealogy and rising from the things of the earth to the things of heaven, while St. John's Gospel starts straight off with Christ as "the Word" in the first verse, "portraying in the higher light of wisdom that radiates from above, out through the lower streams of knowledge, with which St. Matthew is more conversant."[145]

So, the gift of wisdom treats of the highest of things, the divine things of God. St. Thomas tells us that although the gifts

[144] *The Theological Virtues*, p. 396.
[145] Ibid.

of knowledge and understanding flow from the theological virtue of faith, the gift of wisdom, the greatest of all the gifts, flows from charity — the greatest of all the virtues (1 Cor. 13:13). As with knowledge and understanding, the intellectual *virtue* of wisdom is built by our efforts and guided by human reason, but like God's other gifts, the *gift* of wisdom is infused in us by the Holy Spirit. It "comes down from above" (James 3:15).

Thomas declares that "wisdom which is a gift, has its cause in the will, which cause is charity, but it has its essence in the intellect, whose act is to judge aright."[146] While the primary act of the intellect is to know the truth, the primary act of the will is to love the good. The gift of wisdom then empowers us through the aid of the Holy Spirit to grasp the highest truths of God of which our minds are capable, prompted by the ardent love of the highest good and source of all good — God! Joy is the emotion we experience when we attain what we love. The gift of wisdom helps us attain union with God in mind and in heart, and it brings with it great joy.

Recall, if you will, this chapter's opening quotations. It happens that the Latin word for wisdom is *sapientia*, a contraction of *sapor*, "taste," "savor," or "flavor," and *scientia*, "science," which suggests that wisdom is a "sweet-tasting science." The psalmist calls us to "taste and see" that the Lord is God. We see God with the light of our intellects and savor Him through the love in our hearts. Clearly then, the gift of wisdom has nothing to do with cold and tasteless abstractions, but is a gift that inflames our minds and hearts through a closer union with the goodness of God, a union we savor and relish. We should want the gift of wisdom so badly that we can taste it!

---

[146] *ST*, II-II, Q. 45, art. 4.

Further, God has directed us to love Him with all that we are and also to love our neighbors as ourselves. The gift of wisdom, although primarily judging of the divine things of God, also has a practical use in that it allows us to judge practical matters from a divine perspective, thereby guiding and ordering our lives so that we may best serve our neighbors, sharing with them the fruits of charity and wisdom.

WELCOME TO THE HOUSE OF WISDOM!

God must certainly want us to dwell in wisdom, for in multiple places in the Bible wisdom is compared to a house. For example, Proverbs 24:3–5 tells us: "By wisdom a house is built, and by understanding it is established; by knowledge the rooms are filled with all precious and pleasant riches. A wise man is mightier than a strong man, and a man of knowledge than he who has strength."

Another such verse that caught the Seraphic Doctor's attention was Proverbs 9:1: "Wisdom has built her house, she has set up her seven pillars." Now, before he supplied his exegesis St. Bonaventure asked an amusing rhetorical question: "But what are the seven pillars of this house? Should I make them up out of my own head?"[147] He answers his question no, because the pillars of wisdom are right there in Sacred Scripture: "But the wisdom from above is first pure, then peaceable, gentle, open to reason, full of mercy and good fruits, without uncertainty or insincerity" (James 3:17). He then expounds on each of the pillars, of which I'll provide just some highlights here:

[147] *Collations*, p. 188.

BONAVENTURE'S SEVEN PILLARS OF WISDOM[148]

1. *Chastity* (purity) is the first pillar, because as is written in Wisdom 1:4: "Wisdom will not enter a deceitful soul, nor dwell in a body enslaved to sin." One example is that of King Solomon, who, although he had been "filled with wisdom like a river" (Sir. 47:14), lost his wisdom because of his lust for women (see Sir. 47:19–21).

2. *Innocence of mind* (peaceable) is wisdom's second pillar, because peace derives from an innocence and humility whereby one submits humbly to those superior in authority, treats peers impartially, and does not take advantage of one's inferiors. Those who love their equals, obey their superiors, and properly rule those who are subject to them find peace. "Who is wise and instructed among you? Let him by his good behavior show his work in the meekness of wisdom" (James 3:13).

3. *Moderation in speech* (gentle) is the third pillar of wisdom, as Sirach 20:7 states: "A wise man will be silent till the right time comes, but a babbler and a fool will not pay attention to the time." Bonaventure elaborates that evil speech kills both the speaker and the listener: "You

---

[148] Please note that, due to slight differences in translation and the fact that St. Bonaventure used a Latin translation, and his words have in turn been translated into English, some of the words he uses for the pillars differ a bit from the RSV translation I provided above, as I'll try to make clear as we move through the pillars by placing the words from the RSV in parentheses.

cannot speak detraction about your neighbor without killing yourself with the same sword."[149]

4. *Docility in affect* (open to reason) is the fourth pillar of wisdom. The wise are willing to learn from others. As Proverbs 9:8 advises: "Do not reprove a scoffer, or he will hate you; reprove a wise man, and he will love you." Bonaventure observes that the wise know their own faults and are displeased with them. Further, when we correct a person and persuade him of the evil of his ways, we have given him a greater favor then if we gave him the whole world.

5. *Generosity in action* (full of mercy and good fruits) is wisdom's fifth pillar. As Bonaventure so pithily puts it: "Wisdom wants to have mercy not only in affect, but in effect as well."[150] Indeed, "from their fruits you shall know them" (see Matt. 7:16, 20). Pulling from a few verses of Proverbs (31:20, 26, 16), Bonaventure notes that those who have opened their mouths to wisdom have the law of mercy on their tongues, open their hands to the poor, and provide them with fruits of their labors.

6. *Maturity of judgment* (without uncertainty) is pillar number six. As Psalm 36:30 relates: "The mouth of the just one will meditate wisdom, and his tongue will speak judgment."[151] A mature judge will zealously approve everything good and disapprove everything

[149] *Collations*, p. 191.
[150] Ibid., p. 193.
[151] RSV = Ps. 37:30: "The mouth of the righteous utters wisdom, and his tongue speaks justice."

evil. When James 2:4 states: "Are you not making distinctions among yourselves and do you not become judges with evil thoughts?" he is not saying that a person should not judge at all, "concerning an issue about which he has certitude, authority, and correct zeal."[152] Rather, he is saying that we should not judge evil to be good and good to be evil, and further, that "a person should be more inclined to excuse kindly than to accuse wrongly." St. Bonaventure, then, believed it is wise in unclear circumstances to think the best of our neighbor and give the benefit of the doubt, rather than imputing their evil intentions or acts. And further, "it is the highest form of foolishness when people judge the personal faults of others and overlook themselves."

7. *Sincerity of intention* (without insincerity) is wisdom's seventh pillar. Bonaventure expounds upon 1 Kings 10:18–19, which describe King Solomon's glorious throne with six steps. Those six steps are like the wisdom's other six pillars that circle around the throne of this last and highest one, for there is one highest all of intentions the wise person will seek with the utmost sincerity, without deceit, hypocrisy, or any duplicity, indeed, with all his heart, mind, and soul. This pillar is revealed in Colossians 3:2–3: "Seek the things that are above, where Christ is seated at the right hand of God. Set your minds on things that are above, not on things that are on earth."

---

[152] *Collations*, p. 196.

Upon the throne of wisdom, then, sits Jesus Christ Him-self. It was also He who advised us to build our own house of wisdom and who is the solid rock that serves as its foundation: "Everyone who hears these words of mine and does them will be like a wise man who built his house upon the rock" (Matt. 7:24). And as for those of us who do embrace Christ, who do as He tells us, and who, with the Holy Spirit's aid, build houses of wisdom on earth, He tells us as well that in the next life, the are many rooms prepared for us in his Father's house (cf. John 14:2).

THE SACRAMENTS OF WISDOM

The wise men and women of the Church, the Fathers and Doc-tors and saints, have examined every virtue, grace, gift, and sac-rament from God from almost every conceivable angle, and St. Thomas tells us that earlier theologians had related each of the sacraments to one of the seven virtues as follows:

> They say that Baptism corresponds to Faith, and is ordained against Original Sin; Extreme Unction, to Hope, being ordained against venial sin; the Eucharist, to Charity, being ordained against the penal effect which is malice; Order, to Prudence, being ordained against igno-rance; Penance to Justice, being ordained against mortal sin; Matrimony to Temperance, being ordained against concupiscence.[153]

Here I've culled out the parallels:

---

[153] *ST*, III, Q. 65, art. 1.

THE SEVEN GIFTS OF THE HOLY SPIRIT

THE SEVEN SACRAMENTS	THE SEVEN VIRTUES
Baptism	Faith
Anointing of the sick	Hope
Eucharist	Charity
Holy Orders	Prudence
Penance	Justice
Confirmation	Fortitude
Matrimony	Temperance

We might meditate on which sacraments seem also to have the closest affinity to each of the seven gifts of the Holy Spirit. Confirmation, as we have noted, bears a special relationship to the gift of fortitude as well as the virtue, since we pray both for fortitude and for a strengthening of all of the gifts in this holy rite. So which sacrament or sacraments might also have a special relationship to the gift of wisdom?

We could surely say that the Eucharist bears a special relationship to wisdom because wisdom is the highest gift that flows from the virtue of charity. In the Eucharist we also set our minds on the highest thing, Christ Himself, Wisdom Incarnate, and are joined with Him in the most intimate of ways. Indeed, after receiving Communion in the Traditional Latin Mass, the priest prays that the body and blood of our Lord that he has received will "*adhaerat visceribus meis*," "cleave to my innermost parts."

Holy Orders should also bear a special relationship to the gift of wisdom, so that the ordained priests who bring us the body, blood, soul, and divinity of Christ can also share with us the wisdom of Christ as they open the Scriptures to us while they explicate the Gospel in their homilies. St. Thomas tells us that the gift of wisdom judges primarily of the divine things of God and then judges the things of the world from that divine perspective. And who is it that we turn to in the most difficult of situations when divine wisdom is most direly needed? "The Universal Church cannot err, since she is governed by the Holy Ghost, Who is the Spirit of Truth."[154] Further, regarding the pope himself, St. Thomas writes, to him belongs "authority which is empowered to decide matters of faith finally, so that they may be held by all with unshakeable faith. Now this belongs to the authority of the Sovereign Pontiff, to whom the more difficult questions that arise in the Church are referred."[155]

FOLLY, FOE OF WISDOM

So what, then, can we do to make sure we are not undermining our own house of wisdom? We saw that the vice of *ignorance* thwarts the gift of knowledge and *hebetude* or *dullness* thwarts the gift of understanding. The vice of *folly* is wisdom's foe. The Scriptures as a whole, and the book of Proverbs in particular, spell out plenty of contrasts between the attitudes, desires, and actions of the wise and those of the foolish. We have discussed

[154] *ST*, I, Q. 1, art. 9.
[155] Ibid., art.10.

many characteristics and behaviors of the wise so far in this chapter. The fool, by contrast, according to Proverbs, rejects reproof and goes astray (10:17), is right in his own eyes (12:15), throws off restraint and is careless (14:16), has a hasty temper (14:29), gives full vent to his anger (29:11), has eyes on the ends of the earth (17:24), takes no pleasure in understanding, but only in his own opinion (18:2), will ever be quarreling (20:3), and repeats his folly "like a dog that returns to its vomit" (26:11).

These characteristics all follow when a person rejects the virtue and the gift of wisdom. Folly, says St. Thomas, "denotes a special dullness of sense in judging, and chiefly regards the highest cause, which is the last end and the sovereign good."[156] Wisdom has its priorities straight and focuses most on the things that truly matter. Wisdom sets priorities, "first things first," especially in the case of the First Cause!

Thomas says we may experience folly for two main reasons. Some small minority of people have mental limitations, whereby they may receive the grace of the gift of wisdom, but because of their deficient cognitive abilities they are not able to reason about the higher things, and there is no sin in that. But far more often the one who embraces folly over wisdom does so "by plunging his sense into earthly things, whereby his sense is rendered incapable of perceiving Divine things according to 1 Cor. 2:14, *The sensual man perceiveth not these things that are of the Spirit of God,* even as sweet things have no savor for a man whose taste is infected with an evil humor: and such like folly is a sin."[157]

The psalmist tells us, "The fool says in his heart, 'There is no God'" (Ps. 14:1). Perhaps some foolish people have the sense in

---

[156] *ST*, II-II, Q. 46, art. 2.
[157] Ibid.

their *minds* to know that God is there, yet because their *hearts* are directed to the things of the earth, their actions speak out as if God did not exist for them. As the God-Man tells us, "For where your treasure is, there will your heart be also" (Matt. 6:21). How much wiser we will be if we come to taste, see, savor, and treasure the good things of God rather than merely the pleasures of our senses.

PRAYING FOR WISDOM

St. Bonaventure links the seventh petition of the Lord's Prayer, "and deliver us from evil," with a prayer for the gift of wisdom, since we cannot conquer evil desires of the flesh without the Holy Spirit's gift of wisdom. Indeed, as we just saw in St. Thomas's explication, we arrive at folly rather than wisdom when we plunge our senses into worldly things, and as St. Paul has told us, "the wisdom of the world is folly with God" (1 Cor. 3:19).

To achieve the gift of wisdom "from above," St. James simply says, "If any of you lack wisdom, let him ask God, who gives to all men generously and without reproaching, and it will be given him" (James 1:5). Let us pray, then, with St. Alphonsus Liguori: "Grant me the spirit of wisdom that I may despise the perishable things of this world and aspire only after things that are eternal."

THE PEACE THAT WISDOM BRINGS

We saw from Bonaventure's exegesis of James 3:17 that to be peaceable is a pillar of wisdom, and St. Thomas explains that from the gift of wisdom flows the seventh beatitude "blessed are the peacemakers, for they shall be called sons of God" (Matt. 5:9). He notes on the *merit* side of the beatitude, citing Augustine's observation that "peace is the tranquility of order,"[158] that a peace-maker produces peace either in himself, or in others, which is the result of setting in proper order all the things required for peace. He cites Aristotle as well, who described a defining characteristic of wisdom as setting things in order. As for the *reward* side of the beatitude, that peacemakers will be called sons of God, Thomas notes that we become children of God by participating in the likeness of his only-begotten son, Jesus Christ, "according to Rom. 3:29: Whom He foreknew ... to be made conformable to the image of His Son, Who is Wisdom Begotten. Hence by participating in the gift of wisdom, man attains to the sonship of God."[159]

Although Thomas did not specifically address the fruits of the gift of wisdom, we may conclude that they coincide with those of the gift of charity, from which the gift flows, including the *joy* that comes from union with the highest object of our love (recall again the *savor* of *sapientia!*), as well as that pillar, beatitude, and also the *fruit* of *peace*.

MARY, *SEDES SAPIENTIAE*

The Blessed Mother was so graced with wisdom that one of her many titles is "Seat of Wisdom," a very ancient title that came to be recited in the sixteenth-century Litany of Loreto, as is the title "Mother of Good Counsel," as was noted in chapter 5. Indeed, the English Dominican Fathers' translation of St. Thomas's *Summa Theologica* from which we have been drawing is dedicated to "the Blessed Virgin Mary Immaculate, Seat of Wisdom."

[158] *ST*, II-II, Q. 45, art. 6.
[159] Ibid.

Mother Mary had often been depicted in statuary and in paintings as seated upon a majestic throne with the child Jesus in her lap. Mary had been likened by medieval theologians to Solomon's throne of wisdom, and Christ was considered Wisdom Incarnate. Therefore, Mary's lap was indeed the seat or throne of wisdom! Through her total submission to and cooperation with the Holy Spirit, she attained to the most intimate union with God, she sheltered Wisdom in her womb and then brought Him forth for all of us. May Mary, Seat of Wisdom, serve as our model and our intercessor so that we too might share it the spirit of the gift of wisdom.

CHRIST, WISDOM INCARNATE

Lastly we come to Wisdom Incarnate, to Christ, who sits in the seat of wisdom, at the right hand of God, who dwells in wisdom's house, lays the foundations for wisdom's pillars, and awaits us at the top of the ladder set up for us by the Holy Spirit's seven gifts, to guide us to the rooms in heaven that He has prepared for us. Christ asks us to taste and see His goodness in the Eucharist and to judge of the things of the earth through the divine wisdom He imparted to us in His sermons, in His parables, and in the wisdom of the Cross.

It is up to us whether we are willing to submit to the stirrings of the Holy Spirit, take up our own crosses and follow Him, so that ultimately, through the infusion of the virtue of charity and the great gift of wisdom, we might become gentle and lowly of heart like Wisdom Incarnate, and might find His yoke is easy and His burden light (Matt. 11:30), and the path that He and His Spirit will guide us along will lead us to the heavenly paradise.

PROFILE IN GIFTEDNESS #7

ST. THOMAS AQUINAS: GOD'S GIFT OF WISDOM TO THE CATHOLIC CHURCH

The pages of this book have drawn so heavily from the heavenly wisdom of the Angelic Doctor that what more is there to say? Not much perhaps, but here we go! If the Scriptures themselves and St. Jerome's Vulgate are among the Holy Spirit's gifts of wisdom that we can hold in our hands, so too is the *Summa Theologica*. The gift of wisdom provides knowledge of divine things whereby we can judge of all things. Carol Robinson, a twentieth-century lay Thomist, once compared studying St. Thomas to climbing a mountain through a path carved out by a powerful intellect: "At the summit is wisdom. Should you attain it you can stand tall and admire God and His greatness. Then you can look down on human affairs and judge them."[160]

St. Thomas helps us stand tall in wisdom, because that is just what he did. His *Summa Theologica* starts at the heights of the majesty of God, follows His work of creation, and judges of the nature of humanity and of human happiness, before pointing to Christ as the only true guide along the path back to God. St. Thomas tasted of the wisdom of God and saw that it was good. When Christ told him in a vision that he had served Him well in his writings, He asked Thomas what he would like as his reward. "Only You, Lord" was his answer.

St. Thomas Aquinas's feast day is January 28.

[160] Carol Robinson, *My Life with Saint Thomas Aquinas* (Kansas City, MO: Angelus Press, 1992), p. 17.

WELCOMING WISDOM

St. Thomas, Angelic Doctor, residing among the choirs of angels and saints, pray for us, so that we may so fully possess the Holy Spirit's gift of wisdom that our hearts and minds will savor divine things and seek only Christ.

ANGELIC ANALYSIS #7

THE GIFTS AND THE FRUITS

The *fruits* of the Spirit are perfections that the Holy Spirit
forms in us as the first fruits of eternal glory. The tradition of the Church lists twelve of them: "charity, joy,
peace, patience, kindness, goodness, generosity, gentle-
ness, faithfulness, modesty, self-control, chastity."

—*Catechism of the Catholic Church*, no. 1832

The beatitudes are acts of virtue: while the
fruits are delights in virtuous acts.

—St. Thomas Aquinas, *Summa Theologica*, II-II, Q. 157, art. 2

The Church's list of the twelve fruits of the Holy Spirit build
upon the list of "fruits of the Spirit" St. Paul provides in Galatians 5:22–23 in contrast with a list of sinful behaviors that are
"the works of the flesh" in verses 19–21.[161] St. Thomas draws our
attention as well to a verse in Revelation "that may be a reference to them: Apoc. 22:2: *On both sides of the river was the tree
of life bearing twelve fruits*."[162]

---

[161] Although the RSV cited above, as well as various other translations, list nine fruits in this verse, the Church's tradition
built upon the twelve fruits listed in St. Jerome's Latin Vulgate
translation, which can also be seen, with minor variations of
the names of some fruits, in the Douay-Rheims translation.
[162] *ST*, I-II, Q. 70, art. 3.

So what exactly are these fruits of the Holy Spirit? To put it in a nutshell (or perhaps, more suitably, a coconut shell), Thomas points out that "the fruits are any virtuous deeds in which one delights."[163] As fruit is produced by the tree, good works are produced by man. As material fruits please and refresh us, so do spiritual fruits, "with a holy and genuine delight." The *gifts* make us receptive to the inspiration of God, so that we may bear (and enjoy) the *fruits*.

FRUITS AND BEATITUDES: WHAT'S THE DIFFERENCE?

So then, the fruits are delights that we take in virtuous acts, especially those acts perfected by the gifts. How, then, do the fruits differ from the Beatitudes? St. Thomas notes that "all beatitudes may be called fruits, but not vice versa." The Beatitudes and the fruits share in common that both are virtuous deeds that bring us delight, but the difference is that "it is sufficient for a fruit to be something ultimate and delightful; whereas for a beatitude, it must be something perfect and excellent."[164] In other words, as natural virtues and gifts are both habits disposing us toward the good, the gifts are superior in that they operate under the guidance of the stirrings of the Holy Spirit. Fruits and beatitudes are both delightful results of meritorious acts, but Beatitudes are more complete and perfect works that provide even higher delights. How delightful that the Giver gives us so many ways to guide us toward happiness, on earth and in heaven.

---

[163] Ibid., art. 2. The words used to list the twelve fruits in the ST, I-II, Q. 70, art. 3 as translated by the Dominican Fathers are as follows: charity, joy, peace, patience, long-suffering, goodness, benignity, meekness, faith, modesty, continency, and chastity.

[164] Ibid.

THE SEVEN GIFTS OF THE HOLY SPIRIT

THE FRUITS THAT FLOW FROM THE GIFTS

We've seen by now that St. Thomas Aquinas was not one to leave any loose ends untied or any potential connections unconnected! He described certain beatitudes that flow from each particular gift, and you may rest assured he did the same in detailing which fruits tend to grow most directly from the nourishment of the gifts.

THE FRUITS THAT FLOW FROM THE GIFTS

GIFT	FRUIT
Fear of the Lord	Modesty, self-control, chastity
Piety	Kindness, generosity
Knowledge	Faithfulness
Fortitude	Patience, gentleness
Counsel	Goodness
Understanding	Faithfulness
Wisdom	Charity, joy, peace

PROFILE IN GRACE #7

ST. PATRICK OF IRELAND: FRUITS WORTH DECADES OF CULTIVATION

The patron saint of Ireland was not Irish, at least not by birth, but the fruits he planted in Irish soils are all still there for the picking. St. Patrick (ca. 387–461) was born at Bannavem Taburniae (the field of the tents) somewhere on the island that now houses England, Scotland, and Wales, and his first extended visit to the island next door to the west was in the role of a slave, courtesy of Irish pirates.

While we are blessed with nearly countless pious legends of St. Patrick's life, we are blessed as well with the pages of his own authentic *Confessio*, wherein he tells the story of his kidnapping and escape. Although he was the son of a deacon, Patrick did not take his Faith seriously until after he was kidnapped before he turned sixteen. While made to tend sheep in the mountains of Ireland, Patrick would pray as often as a hundred times per day and as many times at night, imploring God for his freedom and deliverance from Ireland, which was not to come for nearly seven years. In his *Confessio* he relates the story of his kidnapping and escape, including his acute awareness of the stirrings of the Holy Spirit. He tells of an incident one night when he saw someone praying, and it was as if Patrick were inside his own body and hearing himself pray above him, above his interior, or inner, man. He prayed powerfully with signs and groans and realized near the end of the prayer that it was the Holy Spirit praying through him. He remembered that St. Paul had written, "the Spirit himself intercedes with us with sighs too deep for words" (Rom. 8:26).

When he returned to Ireland, St. Patrick must have demonstrated all of the succulent fruits of the Holy Spirit for virtually the whole island nation to reject the gods of their ancestors and accept the Triune God whom he taught them about. Perhaps one fruit in which St. Patrick grew most abundantly was *patience*, rendered perhaps even better in his case by the old word *longanimity* or *long-suffering*. Although St. Patrick had prayed for nearly seven years to escape from Ireland, in his *Confessio*, in merely the third sentence after describing his return home, he writes of his burning desire to go back and bring Christ's gospel message to Ireland.

Still, and here is where the fruit of longanimity really comes in, because Patrick was kidnapped as a young man, it took him decades to complete his education, become a priest, then a bishop, achieve papal endorsement, and assemble a team that could build up in Ireland the one, holy, catholic, and apostolic Church (along with scores of physical wooden churches to house a whole island of new priests and parishioners). Indeed, the great saint who converted Ireland did not go back there and really get down to business until he was in his forties or fifties, but powered as he was by the gifts of the Holy Spirit, that did not slow him down.

St. Patrick's feast day is, well, on St. Patrick's Day, of course, March 17.

> *St. Patrick, pray for us, that the Holy Spirit might*
> *sigh and groan through us, strengthening our gifts*
> *and yielding all the sweet fruits, including*
> *longanimity — regardless of how long it might take.*

CONCLUSION

IT IS BETTER TO "RE-GIFT" THAN TO RECEIVE

When in our prayers we ask for things concerning our salvation, we conform our will to God's, of Whom it is written (1 Timothy 2:4) that "*He will have all men to be saved.*"

—St. Thomas Aquinas, *Summa Theologica*, II-II, Q. 83, art. 5

It is more blessed to give than to receive.

—Acts 20:35

ORDERING INSTRUCTIONS

Surely by now we can appreciate the priceless spiritual value of the seven gifts of the Holy Spirit. We have looked at ways in which we can dispose, submit, or surrender ourselves to the Holy Spirit, that we might be made movable by His stirrings, through coming to understand each gift better. We have tried to understand better how to avoid blocking the gifts' reception and actions through our own faults, how the gifts are passed on or strengthened through the sacraments, and how we might petition God for them in prayer, so that we might possess beatitudes and fruits, as did our models and benefactors, Blessed Mother Mary and the Lord Jesus Christ. In concluding I'd like to offer a suggestion as to how you might put all of those surrender plans into action within a particular time-limited prayerful strategy, which some devout readers might surmise will cover the course of nine days.

NINE DAYS OF PRAYER FOR THE *SACRUM SEPTANARIUM*

The basis of this strategy is found in the Scriptures and was taught by Christ Himself, when He asked His disciples to pray and await in Jerusalem the coming of the Holy Spirit on the day of Pentecost. And then, as the disciples, including Blessed Mary, prayed in the Upper Room, the Holy Spirit descended upon them, this time not like a "still, small voice," but like "the rush of a mighty wind" (Acts 2:2) from heaven, and in tongues of fire. And St. Peter preached to the crowd that they were witnessing the prophecy of Joel: "I will pour out my Spirit upon all flesh" (Acts 2:17).

Indeed, the only formal *novena* (nine days of prayer) officially prescribed by the Catholic Church is the Novena to the Holy Spirit for the Seven Gifts prayed in the days leading to Pentecost (fifty days after Ascension Thursday[165] and forty days after Easter). The full procedure and text of the prayers may be easily found online,[166] and I might suggest that on Day 1, we might also do spiritual reading about the Holy Spirit and about the seven gifts in general, for example, in Angelic Analysis essays 2 and 5 of this book or in the corresponding questions of the *Summa Theologica*, the locations of which were provided in the introduction. As you progress on Days 3 through 8, the prayers of the novena could be supplemented with additional readings on the particular gift prayed for each day as found within these chapters, the *Summa Theologica*, St. Bonaventure's *Collations on the Seven Gifts of the Holy Spirit* or other books cited within these pages or discovered on your own. On Day 9, the Vigil of Pentecost, we pray especially for the Holy Spirit's fruits.

THE EVERLASTING VALUE AND JOY OF "RE-GIFTING"

We come now in these bottom lines of this book to the bottom line, so to speak. The gifts of the Holy Spirit are invaluable gifts

---

[165] *Pentecost* being Greek for "fiftieth."

[166] For example, https://www.ewtn.com/devotionals/pentecost/seven.htm.

from heaven that will help us get there and that will remain with us there in eternity. Hear St. Thomas, echoing the teacher of St. Augustine: "Ambrose says, (*De Spiriti Sancto i. 20*): *The city of God, the heavenly Jerusalem is not washed with the waters of an earthly river: it is the Holy Ghost, of Whose outpouring we but taste, Who, proceeding from the Fount of life, seems to flow more abundantly in those celestial spirits, a seething torrent of sevenfold heavenly virtue.*"[167] There, in heaven, when we receive that ultimate gift of beatific vision and union in love with the Triune God, who is Love, the gifts will remain with us forever in their perfected celestial state, eternally refreshing us, with all the Communion of Saints, in their eternal life-giving flow.

Christ taught us to love and that it is better to give than to receive. We cannot give to another person the seven gifts because they are only the Holy Spirit's to give. He will give them to whoever sincerely asks for them, though, and this is where we might play our part. By living our lives through the grace of these gifts, displaying the love, savor, and joy that flows from them, and sharing their succulent fruits with our neighbors, perhaps our neighbors will be prompted to call out from the depths of their heart, "*Veni, Sancte Spiritus!*" (Come, Holy Spirit!)

---

[167] *ST*, II-II, Q. 58, art. 6.

APPENDIX

THE ANGELIC DOCTOR'S QUICK GUIDE TO THE GIFTS[168]

GIFT OF THE HOLY SPIRIT	BRIEF DESCRIPTION
Fear of the Lord	"The gift of fear has for its principal object God, Whom it avoids offending." (II-II, Q. 141, art. 1)
Piety	"Piety, whereby we pay worship and duty to God as our Father, is a gift of the Holy Ghost." (II-II, Q. 121, art. 1)
Knowledge	"Knowledge of human things is called knowledge," and regarding matters of faith, "to know what one ought to believe belongs to the gift of knowledge." (II-II, Q. 9, art. 2)
Fortitude	"Fortitude as a virtue, perfects the mind in the endurance of all perils whatever; but it does not go so far as to give confidence of overcoming all dangers; this belongs to the fortitude that is a gift of the Holy Ghost." (II-II, Q. 139, art. 1)

[168] "The gifts are perfections of man, whereby he becomes amenable to the promptings of the Holy Ghost." *ST*, II-II, Q. 68, art. 3.

APPENDIX

GIFT OF THE HOLY SPIRIT	BRIEF DESCRIPTION
Counsel	"Human reason is unable to grasp the singular and contingent things which may occur," so our counsels are fearful and uncertain, hence, "in the search of counsel man requires to be directed by God who comprehends all things; and this is done through the gift of counsel." (II-II, Q. 52, art. 1)
Understanding	"Man needs a supernatural light, in order to penetrate further still, so as to know what it cannot know by its natural light; and this supernatural light which is bestowed on man is called the gift of understanding." (II-II, Q. 8, art. 1)
Wisdom	"The knowledge of Divine things is called wisdom," and regarding matters of faith, "to know them in themselves, by a kind of union with them, belongs to the gift of wisdom. (II-II, Q. 9, art. 2) "Wisdom as a gift is more excellent than wisdom as an intellectual virtue, since it attains to God more intimately by a kind of union of the soul with Him, it is able to direct us not only in contemplation, but in action." (II-II, Q. 45, art. 4)

THE SEVEN GIFTS OF THE HOLY SPIRIT

HUMAN POWERS, ACTIONS, AND THEIR PERFECTING GIFTS

POWER	HUMAN ACTIONS	PERFECTING GIFTS
Speculative Intellect	Apprehension of truth	Understanding
	Judgment concerning truth	Wisdom
Practical Intellect	Apprehension of truth	Knowledge
	Judgment concerning truth	Counsel
Will	Matters relating to others	Piety
Irascible Appetite	Matters relating to oneself regarding fears of danger	Fortitude
Concupiscible Appetite	Matters relating to oneself regarding inordinate lusts	Fear of the Lord

APPENDIX

THE SERAPHIC DOCTOR UNWRAPS THE GIFTS IN THE LORD'S PRAYER

PETITIONS OF THE LORD'S PRAYER	GIFTS OF THE HOLY SPIRIT
Our Father, who art in heaven, hallowed be Thy name.	Fear of the Lord
Thy kingdom come.	Piety
Thy will be done on earth as it is in heaven.	Knowledge
Give us this day our daily bread.	Fortitude
And forgive us our trespasses as we forgive those who trespass against us.	Counsel
And lead us not into temptation.	Understanding
But deliver us from evil.	Wisdom

THE SEVEN GIFTS OF THE HOLY SPIRIT

THE SEVEN DEADLY SINS MEET MORE THAN
THEIR MATCH IN THE SEVEN HOLY GIFTS[169]

DEADLY SINS	GIFTS OF THE HOLY SPIRIT	EXPLANATION
Sloth	Wisdom	St. Thomas explains that sloth is opposed to the joy of charity about the divine good, and it opposes the Great Commandment to love God with all that we are. Charity is the highest virtue that seeks union with God. The theological virtue of wisdom flows from the virtue of charity, and the intellectual virtue of wisdom is the highest of the intellectual virtues. Wisdom actively seeks out and savors the highest of all causes, which is God.

[169] St. Thomas did not spell out all these parallels, which are merely the author's speculations. Further, as Thomas has noted, the gifts are "connected." They cooperate in various ways to double, triple, and even seven-team, so to speak, all manners of vice and sin. Perhaps you might have some other insights of your own (or better yet, courtesy of the stirrings of the Holy Spirit)!

DEADLY SINS	GIFTS OF THE HOLY SPIRIT	EXPLANATION
Envy	Piety	Envy opposes the joy of charity about our neighbor's good and opposes the second Great Commandment, to love our neighbor as ourselves. The virtue of piety is related to justice, giving each what is his due. Through the gift of piety, we honor God, especially as Father. This means our neighbors are our brothers and sisters in Christ. We share in any of their merits and should rejoice and not be saddened when good things happen to others. In fact, we should pray that they do.
Avarice	Knowledge	Avarice is an inappropriate valuing and love of material goods. The gift of knowledge pertains to true judgment of human things, by which we judge money only as a means, never an end in itself.
Vainglory (and Pride)	Understanding	Per Thomas, the virtue of understanding "is a certain knowledge that penetrates into the heart of things." Through the gift of understanding, the Holy Spirit guides us to grasp the nature of our weakness, fallenness, and dependence on God, instilling within us humility.

THE SEVEN GIFTS OF THE HOLY SPIRIT

DEADLY SINS	GIFTS OF THE HOLY SPIRIT	EXPLANATION
Gluttony	Fortitude	Fortitude enables us to overcome difficult obstacles. When guided by the gift of fortitude, we can overcome the perceived pains and discomfort that come from denying ourselves food or drink beyond what we truly need to keep up our strength.
Lust	Fear of the Lord	As St. Thomas notes, the fear of the Lord is principally concerned with not offending God and fleeing from whatever offends Him. This fear restrains the soul from the wanton concupiscence of inappropriate sexual desires and acts.
Wrath	Counsel	Wrath involves a swelling of the mind with anger that clouds reason. With the gift of counsel, we act not according to our own hot-headed passion, but under the cool guidance of the Holy Spirit, so that true wrongs may be redressed in ways that do not produce further damage.

KEVIN VOST

Kevin Vost (b. 1961) holds a Doctor of Psychology in Clinical Psychology (Psy.D.) degree from Adler University in Chicago. He has taught at Aquinas College in Nashville, the University of Illinois at Springfield, MacMurray College, and Lincoln Land Community College. He has served as a research review committee member for American Mensa, a society promoting the scientific study of human intelligence, and as an advisory board member for the International Association of Resistance Trainers, an organization that certifies personal fitness trainers.

Dr. Vost is the author of over a dozen Catholic books, has appeared on hundreds of Catholic radio and television broadcasts, and has traveled across the United States and Ireland, giving talks on the themes of his books. When home, he continues to drink great drafts of coffee while studying timeless, Thomistic tomes in the company of his wife, their two sons, and their two dogs, in Springfield, Illinois.

Sophia Institute

Sophia Institute is a nonprofit institution that seeks to nurture the spiritual, moral, and cultural life of souls and to spread the Gospel of Christ in conformity with the authentic teachings of the Roman Catholic Church.

Sophia Institute Press fulfills this mission by offering translations, reprints, and new publications that afford readers a rich source of the enduring wisdom of mankind.

Sophia Institute also operates two popular online Catholic resources: CrisisMagazine.com and CatholicExchange.com.

Crisis Magazine provides insightful cultural analysis that arms readers with the arguments necessary for navigating the ideological and theological minefields of the day. *Catholic Exchange* provides world news from a Catholic perspective as well as daily devotionals and articles that will help you to grow in holiness and live a life consistent with the teachings of the Church.

In 2013, Sophia Institute launched Sophia Institute for Teachers to renew and rebuild Catholic culture through service to Catholic education. With the goal of nurturing the spiritual, moral, and cultural life of souls, and an abiding respect for the role and work of teachers, we strive to provide materials and programs that are at once enlightening to the mind and ennobling to the heart; faithful and complete, as well as useful and practical.

Sophia Institute gratefully recognizes the Solidarity Association for preserving and encouraging the growth of our apostolate over the course of many years. Without their generous and timely support, this book would not be in your hands.

www.SophiaInstitute.com
www.CatholicExchange.com
www.CrisisMagazine.com
www.SophiaInstituteforTeachers.org

Sophia Institute Press® is a registered trademark of Sophia Institute.
Sophia Institute is a tax-exempt institution as defined by the
Internal Revenue Code, Section 501(c)(3). Tax I.D. 22-2548708.